A
SINGULAR
COUNTRY

A
SINGULAR
COUNTRY

J.P. DONLEAVY

W · W · NORTON & COMPANY · NEW YORK · LONDON

Copyright © 1989 by J.P. Donleavy
Photography copyright © 1989 by Patrick Prendergast.
First American Edition, 1990.

All rights reserved.
Printed in the United States of America.

Library of Congress Cataloging-in-Publication Data
Donleavy, J.P. (James Patrick), 1926–
A singular country / J.P. Donleavy.
p.   cm.
1. Ireland—Social life and customs—20th century.   I. Title.
DA959.1.D66   1990
941.5082—dc20
89–29926

ISBN 0-393-02760-0

W.W. Norton & Company, Inc., 500 Fifth Avenue, New York, N.Y. 10110
W. W. Norton & Company, Ltd., 37 Great Russell Street, London WC1B 3NU

1 2 3 4 5 6 7 8 9 0

A
SINGULAR
COUNTRY

THE WORLD OF IRELAND LETS HIM LIE WHERE THE

RAIN FALLS BUT RARELY DOES THE DUBLIN GREEN

GIVE A MAN A DRY PLACE TO SLEEP. BUT

WHOMEVER HE MAY BE YOU CAN BE SURE HE

RESTS IN PEACE.

A
SINGULAR
COUNTRY

From Oola to Knocknabooley, and Doohama to Ballyshoneen you'd only just know by the last mentioned name that you weren't in Asia but in the land of saints and scholars. But in the directions that most of these location signs point you might be less lost if you were halfway up some deep gulch in the foothills of Tibet. For the natives still faithfully play their little trick of sending the visiting stranger in the wrong heading. But always with the friendly intention that he would not miss the most welcome views of this countryside. So if for any reason you really need to get where you are going it is prudent to never be without your flashlight, your ordnance survey map and your compass.

Ah but one thing you can always be sure of, the silver streams pouring their glistening waters down brown boggy mountainsides or the grass bejeweled with moisture drops under these greyest of grey skies will tell you with rainbows ablaze, that it is in Ireland you are and it is there that you are closest of all to heaven. And to a smiling benign god who sports a thick Irish brogue. For the shores of this singular country extend out beyond its surrounding seas to the distant rest of the world where these Irish have gone over the centuries and, far from their native soil, have in their new generations continued to dream of that sacred emerald realm left behind.

There remains always a consciousness in the Irish mind that this is a land where no man is utterly friendless and where no corpse goes to its grave without mourners. And where the human condition no matter how forlorn or reprehensible can always trust to find a smile, or a kind word or helping hand. And never mind the occasional marauder with drink taken and lurching shouting down the main street of a town who might put his fist through an occasional pane of glass or try to throttle a tourist. Without a paintbrush, easel or a typewriter and paper he's merely giving artistic expression to his being, in the only way he knows how. And in this latter endeavour he's a perfectionist.

But you would be grievously wrong to think Ireland is one of the most dangerous countries in the world. For such disorderly spoilers so ranting and raving and in such a condition as to be a source of danger to pedestrian and vehicular traffic, are often actually on their way to play pop with and kick in the door of the local Garda station. As this preceding place is usually situated centrally and prominently in the town you'd be wise to view the ensuing embranglement at a safe distance, preferably an unobtrusive doorway down a side street. But take comfort from the fact that Guards in Ireland are notoriously tall and strong and despite their normally kindly and gentle manners, it will not deter them in dragging the culprit off the public highway and throwing this awful belligerent eegit into a cell. But do be mindful that the customarily somnolent Irish country town is enlivened by such breaches of the peace. For your man meant no real harm other than to let citizens know, he was, like anybody else, full of human frailties and was in town having a bit of a jar and enjoying himself.

For in truth Ireland is from one coast to another chock a block full of fine decent people, who although they are capable of putting you accidentally to death, would never countenance doing so deliberately, and never is there any doubt that permanent harm was meant. And so provided the marauder hasn't suffered total memory loss, and if you've been a tourist caught in the melée, his remorse and sincerest sympathy will be expressed when he comes to see you in your hospital bed and examines the fingerprints he left on your windpipe. And if the very worst has happened you can be sure he'll be present with other mourners at your newly purchased grave site. And believe one thing, there is hardly anywhere left in the world to give you a better funeral and that, preceded by a gleeful wake.

Which would put
Upon your face
A permanent smile
As you rest
In peace.

DEATH IS AN IMPORTANT SOCIAL OCCASION FOR
THE LIVING AS WELL AS THE DECEASED. TRIBUTES
ARE GENEROUS BUT LITTLE IS EVER NEEDED TO
MARK AN IRISH GRAVE WHERE MEMORIES STAY
LONG ALIVE.

II

And here one is upon a morning in the midlands of this
country in a chipper mood on the brightest of bright
breezy November days, hiding my notebook from the wind
on a railroad station platform and starting to write these
words while waiting for a friend to arrive on the train.
Fresh clean clouds sweeping across the sky with a sweet air
lightly gusting up from the south east. A clink and clang of
men leisurely hammering spikes into the railroad tracks.
And amid the pigeons and jackdaws criss crossing the sky,
flocks of smaller birds are rendezvouing over this midlands
Irish conurbation. For here in this town of Mullingar the
tracks divide to go westwards, left to Galway and right to
Sligo. And such a consequential junction has led to momen-
tous things. For there is an architectural splendour to be
found here, as well as an astonishing engineering feat not
often to be seen outside Dublin town. Steps lead down to a
commodious tunnel built under the very tracks. And above

rises a Georgian bow fronted building whose graceful elevation and grey lichen spotted granite colour glowing bright in the sunshine, makes this station memorably pleasant and modestly magnificent.

One might uncharitably say all this is what the Protestant English settlers left behind as they fled the turmoil of the political and social struggle which has existed since in the most of holy Catholic Ireland. But the Catholic religion too has brought magnificence to this town. To the north of this station, the clock at the top of a twin towered cathedral sparkles gold as its bells toll eleven and proclaims a soaring glory on the skyline. And one is reminded by the train's whistle far out on the bog lands that there is no strife in this present silence. As now one waits for the throbbing diesel to emerge into sight around the curving track, having, as it has, crossed that great haunting heather blanketed stretch of land called the Bog of Allen. A mystically bleak sad terrain memorably mentioned in the closing words of James Joyce's story "The Dead".

As the great weight of the train's locomotive pounds into the station it makes the platform tremble. The carriages are nationalistically orange and white, their windows adorned with 'No Smoking' stickers. The train's engineer has thrown a key ring out to the station master as he in turn holds another to be shoved up on the train engineer's arm. An impeccably smooth demonstration of safety. For this exchange makes it foolproof that this present train will be the only one proceeding further on this single track to Sligo and will not be met head on by another coming the other way. Which some uncharitable persons might think to be an expected Gaelic situation. But of course had you been a passenger on the train you'd wonder. For as you left the station in Dublin and were now a mile or two out with gravestones of Glasnevin cemetery flashing by the window and cruising comfortably at your usual twenty five knots, there comes an announcement loud and clear over the tannoy.

"For the benefit of those travellers who are on the wrong train and who want to proceed to Belfast this is to inform them that this is the train to Sligo."

Ah but this is Ireland where your own damn fault always has a damn good chance of succeeding. And the point is what's your hurry. And inconvenience be damned. Why not go a long way out of your way and take a journey to a place where you've never been before and had certainly never intended of ever going. And there totally cut off from your previous troubles, be stranded a few slowly pass-ing hours in a fuming rage until finally forced to have an intoxicating drink at one of the many fine pubs they have in the town. Or indeed in the case of Mullingar, to be able to go visit the world's most astonishing hotel decoration, the wax effigy of James Joyce himself sitting crossed legged in a pair of plimsolls reading a book inside a glass case in the sedate Greville Arms Hotel. So let me tell you, you could do much worse than ending up stuck in the various prosperous midland towns. But of course when the telephone doesn't work, each one more fucked up than the last, after you've walked a mile and tried three, soon you're leaping up and down the pavement and glowering at every passerby since it's utterly clear to you now that you won't be able to tell those waiting for you in Belfast that you won't be there soon. And just there in front of you is a car parked with a sticker on its rear window which says "I love New York."

And it's in that latter city with its marvellously working telephones on numerous street corners, where presently you wouldn't mind being. But on this island where down the road means up the road and up the road means down, at least you're quickly learning to be ready for surprises and to keep your options open. Which I was reminding myself to do moving out my front gates just outside this midland town to head south west towards the mini metropolis of Tullamore. And one did not have to travel far to come across further evidence of the typical eccentricities and glowering revenges that can possess this land. For just south west of Mullingar you arrive at one of Ireland's more astonishing edifices, reputed to be the largest folly in the country, and still raging immovable in its silent proclamation to this day. Called the Jealous Wall, this masonry monument in the gardens of Belvedere House rises just inland from the shores of Lough Ennel. And out of the trees it looms to a magnificent height, built to blot out another and nearby country house on the landscape. And what better or more lasting purpose could any wall ever serve, giving splendid evidence of the entrenched antagonism and repugnance that can eternally glower across this shamrock green land.

However, you'd think the major significance of this huge edifice would have now, with its protagonists, faded as their bones have into history. You'd only nearly be half right. For on today's Irish landscape the natives practise an inverse variation of the Jealous Wall. By first ripping out the blackthorn, ash, bramble and holly from the ancient hedgerow before levelling it to the ground. And then building a residence conspicuously to be seen from the road. This in order to put their passing neighbours into a permanent state of seething and boiling envy. The glass of every window polished clean and clear so that the glint in the eye of the ceramic leprechauns perched inside on the shiny veneer of the coffee table, can't be missed. And naturally, what else would you expect of the innocent passerby, left feeling awfully inferior having just hand milked his cow, the warm pail hanging at his side, and with the rain dripping through the thatch of his cottage and the turf smoke curling up from his cooking fire staining his encrusted lime white washed walls. Had this small farmer the money of this petrol station owner, he'd soon too build an even more conspicuous house even closer to the road and festooned it would be with the latest in architectural pretensions of your multi coloured stonework around the entrance porch. And now that there's a computer or two in the country, you'd even be witnessing remote controlled dancing tassels on the window shades. Not to mention the plastercast life sized eagles, wings outstretched, that would knock your hat off as they sit on the verge of going air-borne either side of the path up to the front door. And let me tell you further that if you press the bell which glows even in the darkest night, you may be sure that that button will be capable of bringing alive chimes in the household to the tune of 'Ave Maria'.

Ah but now the real culprit of all of this edifice embellishment which puts the plain neighbour to shame is your American and Australian T.V. serials showing your casual open plan suburbia with your neighbours without so much as a warning shout across the lawn, walking into the kitchen door of your house as if it were theirs and then having the crass audacity of looking to see what you've got in your refrigerator. And not even washing away the imprint of their lips from the carton of milk they take a drink from. Can there be any doubt that these signal examples of North American and Australian life should be banned from beaming down out of the innocent skies of Ireland.

Yet now, is too late. These unmistakable accumulating blemishing structures decorate the outskirts of every Irish town and village from one corner end of Ireland to the other. But along with the gasps of horror at last admonishing hands have been raised. And an attempt or two made to blot out the offending abode with a hedge or cover of thatch, or a splash of a white wash. But it will be a long time before we ever get back to a good old mud wall or two. And for the sensitive eye wanting somewhere to safely look to put such show offs out of sight where they mercifully and tastefully belong, you'd be erecting a Jealous Wall twice as long as the Great Wall of China. But bejabbers, time has a way of proving one wrong. And I'm certain in the usual one hundred and twenty years it takes, such bungalows and bijou split level ranch houses, with their cathedral arched and stained glass windows plus the window shade tassels dancing, will become the rage and sought after by the architectural aficionados of the future, searching as they will be for the most authentic pebble dashed breeze block edifice for which to slap down their money and into which they will smugly ensconce themselves. And making every visiting American and Australian architectural scholar pull their forelock as they humbly approach up the garden path between the leprechaun statuary with camera and notebook in hand to ask if they may photograph the interior adornments and the elevations.

Now you may be wondering why all this is said about

Ireland. When by god, there are no end of unsightly shacks out in the rest of the world with your disgracefully execrable examples of bad taste being perpetrated and folk teaching the landscape an ugly lesson it won't forget. And the reason is that Eire is above all an agricultural community which hitherto had wrought no disgrace upon the small face it shows upon this earth having as it has decent looking cattle, horses, sheep and pigs roaming nearly every bit of the landscape. Although it's admitted there are a few other inhabited similar areas of the globe, surely the rural highways and byways of Ireland were before the advent of television the world's most unspoilt. But now this country holds the world's record for the most systematically continued ruination of some of the most beautiful scenery God, recognizing the unique devoutness of the people, put specially there. And here and now one must coin the words upon which to cast such blame. It is with the 'bijou bungalow blight'. This architectural disease which has spread like wildfire across the length and breadth of the nation and is caught by the victim as they catch envious sight of such brand new elevation along the roadside and plan to do them one better.

In passing, I suppose it is appropriate too to note another side of the coin. That could, were the subject of it unleashed, set matters to right. It is that the Irish are also the world's recognized if not esteemed champions in the business of demolition. Their efficiency and speed in such being mind boggling. Take now a concert grand piano, shining in its mint condition as it innocently stands there able to produce its perfectly tuned dulcet notes. And then enter your team of proven beyond doubt Irishmen. Pick axes, crowbars and sledgehammers over their shoulders at the ready. The gang of them to let fly as you stand there with your stop watch poised at zero seconds and shout "Go". And by god it's not that many tick tocks later that surrounding you and scattered everywhere in your smallest of smithereens is your previous piano with not a particle left that you could even remotely identify as ever having been a fraction of a musical instrument.

Now there's a reason if not a rhyme why all of this is so. You see, the foreigner was at the root of it. Arriving as he did, as the landlord settler. And with his fine manners and upstart pretensions plus a nice parcel of land mapped out, he built himself soaring castles and commodious mansions and populated them with the local Irish servant who was more than eager to have food, shelter and a steady pittance in return for waiting upon your arriviste aristocrat hand and foot. Ah but then, as the not always mild but usually moist gales continued to blow in from the Atlantic and the somber landscape stared back at him along with the sullen eyes of the natives who with their simple primitive ways, left goodly smears of grease on the bottom of the breakfast tray and baked potatoes black and lurked lazily having tea in the mansion's kitchen, it was not long before your upper cruster decided to seek the calmer comforts and sophisticated serenity of where he hailed from in the first place. And so there came into being your plethora of absentee landlords. But this departure was usually felt by the natives to be good riddance to this brief interloper. And by god did they then delve into the butter, tea, bread, jam, ham and eggs not to mention penetrating deep beyond the thick oak door of the wine cellar.

Ah but not all of your arriviste aristocrats were inclined to go. So now let's instead concentrate on your invariably tweedy man who remained. And who was another kettle of philosophical fish entirely. Now perhaps surprisingly, there were more than a few of this kind of chap who came to tolerate it here. Indeed some even liked it and preferred it to England. Usually such a chap had practised and perfected and had handy a stage Irish brogue to use in his occasional banter with the household and estate staff who would be well known not to do anything too quickly or at all if addressed in the superior tones of an English accent.

"Ah begorra Paddy now how do them cattle faring over beyond?"

"Sir I have just this second every last one of them counted and there be not a bother on them. There'd only be two heifers or is it the three, gone missing."

Now of course with the latter bad news from Paddy, your squire would lapse instantly into his best Royal Navy lingo as to where the bloody hell were the two missing heifers. But otherwise your squire man, as Paddy scratched his skull, would remain the benign landlord and mostly uncomplainingly tolerant of the foibles of this indigenous race. Who interpret their oft told lies as being the truth only told for the time being. And sure they didn't mind braiding the mane of your horse till midnight or polishing the hooves of your man's steed at dawn for the day's hunting ahead of the fox. Or them down in the kitchens making a sandwich or two to fit snugly in your silver sandwich box along with polishing, sampling and filling your brandy flask. Or the same if your man set out to shoot pheasant or to loose many a barrel trampling his boggy wastes bang, bang at the elusive snipe darting up. And when not busy with his shotgun out on the miles of bogs he'd row out on one of his lakes to be yanking out the trout. Or with

A SINGULAR COUNTRY

Paddy leading him to the best pools to take salmon out of the river. Or pike out of the lake that do be eating the trout. And prior to and following such sport, your gentleman up in the big house, as he would now be widely known and referred to, would enjoy his Madeira, claret and port. And if a sudden chill was coming on, he would not hesitate to have a few belts of whiskey in between to keep warm. And in this pursuit of such sporting and occasionally comfortable habits, your indigenous Anglo Irishman came to be born. Such gentleman was not inclined to take much notice of his staff robbing him blind. For at least there always seemed a bullock or two left from those gone missing, that could be sent to market. And in the more dire event that there weren't, there were still a few acres that could be sold to the neighbouring farmer. But even before that was done, a few trees out of the plantation of oaks out of sight beyond the hill would bring in a quid or two. For they were growing quick enough in the favourable climate. But never would the sacrilege be committed of taking axe or saw to those trees decorating his parklands and pleasure gardens, or those sheltering him and his mansion from sight along the road. And wherever you see soaring boughs keeping the sun from sweetening the grass you'd know an Anglo Irishman was not far away. So for the present could this squire preserve his endless time being. And do so without having to plumb the depths of what might be a non existent fortune.

But even when there are no more cattle, trees or land to be sold and you yourself up in the big house are going rapidly native in the serenity of the Irish countryside, the days in your life do be flying by like lightning and your feet do tip toe unnoticed towards your grave always nicely situated down its peacefully sylvan dell. And if the natives haven't crept close by moonlight to deliberately put a torch to your mansion or a servant accidentally drop a red hot glowing ember in one of your turf baskets, then only time itself will imperceptibly bring upon you hard times with the usual slate slippings, blocked gutters and downspouts and the roof beams rotting overhead. As you in your trusty, if threadbare, satin smoking jacket, go with your crystal decanter of port, having moved your comfortable sofa and bed to drier rooms, where now, as you quaff your vintages, you avoid the heavier drips of moisture descending from the ceiling.

In all this previous declining time one fact is forever salient. The Irish neighbouring farmer has his gimlet eye on you. He has all along been cunningly letting his own cattle break through your fences to graze every green nibble off your remoter fields. Of course in such winter days it is already too dark by the time you dislodge from bed to exercise your hunting horse out to where the intrusion can be seen. But don't worry, soon your neighbouring farmer will have his cattle brazenly out tearing the emerald blades of grass off the big house park lands and soon after, in fact upon the day of your most exasperated pained complaint, will offer to buy the land at a knockdown price. And why not. You'd still be gentry. And such a convenient arrangement could mean years yet for you peacefully up in the big house allowing you to gracefully pursue your comfortable habits by retaining a paddock or two to graze your hunting horses plus retain the sporting rights over your previous land which would allow you still to hunt, shoot and fish and be surrounded by your flea bitten dogs peeing up against all four posts of your bed. And never mind that now you be digging your meals out of a sardine can with an old rusted wood chisel.

So god forbid should the last examples of this gone native landlord gentleman be taken for his ultimate journey and finally vanish entirely from the last room of his house. The mood of the landscape would surely be poorer without him. But alas more to hear their clipped vowels or to see them in their libraries reading the Daily Telegraph. Not that you would dare brave the four giant Irish wolfhounds to get that close to the window anyway, such faithful dogs being used by Irish kings to smell out traitors in their camp. However, what now. Your man of the gentry is finally laid deep mouldering under the daffodils. Well let me tell you for a start, what now. What use is the big old crumbling mansion to any local farmer or even his hard working wife if she had the nerve to put on such airs and weather the scorn of the neighbours. She'd at the outset need a raincoat for the roof leaks in the kitchen and roller skates to cover the back and forth miles in the hallways. Plus a tiara to wear of an evening down the main staircase on the way to dinner. So in his wellington boots your farmer climbs the granite steps and opens up the front double doors wide to let his cattle in. And here on the parquet floors these beasts have somewhere to scratch themselves on the marble mantels of the chimney pieces and in the commodious reception rooms to be sheltering out of the chill wind and cold rain and not lose a pound or two of flesh that such inclemency would melt off them.

Ah but then as the cow flop goes plop on such mansion's floors and the mooing of the farmer's beasts reverberates through where once the locals were in fear to tread, so too are we left with the ghosts of many of the Anglo

Irish. Whose spirits still dwell here and can make the hair stand up on the back of your head. For on some wild Irish winter nights with gales blowing storm force and rain pelting down, you will see up there on the hill candle light faintly glowing. On this blackest of black evenings. And up there beyond, away within a broken window in the mansion's ballroom, chandeliers glisten and long tables hold silver trays of canapés and great crystal bowls sparkle with punch and champagne. Servants in their moss green livery glide to and fro. And listen. Above the thrashing wind and lashing rain. Do you hear that music? The harp, the viola and the violins. It would be your usual Hungarian orchestra imported all the way by rail and sea from Budapest and playing this waltz. And there be himself enthralled, the gentleman squire, impeccably accoutred in white tie and tails. Protestant angel wings sprouting from his back to flutter from each shoulder blade. Taking the first lady in her flowing long gown of crinolines and silks out to dance across the parquet floor. And lurking near, retainers pull forelocks and bow and scrape. While the fox the master of the household would be hunting in the morning, canine paws on the sill, is peering in through the window. And you might say it was grand, grand, grand. And that all that now is gone, gone, gone. But you would be

Wrong

Wrong

Wrong.

SUCH ANCIENT MONUMENTS WORN BY TIME AND
RAIN STAND IN WITNESS AND REMIND AS DOES
THE STONE OF WHICH THEY ARE, THAT YOU LIVE
ONLY BRIEF SECONDS OF A LIFE.

III

It is time now to get it firmly established in your mind that Ireland is more upper cruster pukka than you think. Not all of your living and breathing ascendancy have disappeared. And more than some little elegance is still hidden under the decay and decline. For there be other settlers who, like their bones in their coffins under the emerald turf, will never vanish from this landscape as so many less resilient of their ilk have, who, clinging to the last shreds of their original magnificence, beat it back to England. For there were some of these folk who had come to love Ireland as their own. And who because of their sympathetic regard and tolerance for the ways of the natives never were totally pilfered into paupery or had their mansions burned. Here and there sheltered back from the roadway they remain upon the landscape, smoke still rising from at least one chimney. Their gateways in their long walls still to be seen. And the squire inhabitant of the big house neither putting a gun to his head nor having to repress the desire to return to the ordered civilisation and safety of the Motherland.

Now His Nib's accent would have long lost its clipped vowels and there would be a soft mellifluousness to his voice. And except for his tailoring, and matched Purdey shotguns and penchant for vintage port, you'd nearly think at a distance he was one of your hand to forelock local natives. And indeed to some considerable extent he is. For hasn't he while maturing to manhood and afterwards, been sowing a few of his wild oats in and among the staff. Now no one is suggesting he couldn't control his healthy outdoor fortified carnal appetites but it would be natural enough for him after some fine dining and wining and a little the worse for port, to be having a go or two at Bridie or Bridget the stout built scullery maids retired after midnight to bed up in their attic cells. And with the consequences arriving like little calves be doing out in the fields, your man wouldn't be thinking any differently about it than he would over the expansion of the numbers in his cattle herd. The increased population simply being there in the household and growing up making themselves as useless as their mothers were and fitting in well with the other staff lurking and lounging around the place. In any event you'd end up having a crew perhaps no better but at least no worse than you'd find in many another Irish country house where the same kind of licentiousness was going on with a gone native Anglo Irish widow or two.

But now as you'd imagine this gentleman and pasha and squire of this great estate is, and has become, a strange specimen indeed. His motto being, hunt, shoot and fish and live and let live. His habit being to turn a blind eye to

malingering, pilfering, trespassing and poaching. And not a
bad word would be said about him by those less materially
endowed who dwelled in the surrounding parish. In fact he
would be referred to as a generous, friendly, decent and
fair man who only had a few screws loose in the head and
perhaps a few bats flying around in his belfry. It being
nearly unanimously agreed that his mansion should be left
standing and he left eating, drinking and even betimes for-
nicating in it. But of course there would always be your
contrary politically motivated nationalists growling discon-
tent, however these usually crackshot and skilled fishermen,
provided they were able to poach a few salmon, rabbits and
pheasant from your man's rivers, forest and parklands
would always hold their agitation till another day.

Now coming out of any reasonable sized town you
don't have to travel far to see such mansion's chimneys
towering on the landscape. And with His Nibs still in it.
The first telltale sign being a stone wall and a plethora of
ancient trees flanking along the road. You'll get some hint
of the owner's financial condition by the number of holes
that falling trees have flattened in the wall. Then soon
you'll come to a gate lodge, tattered curtains behind its
broken windows and with a tree growing through the roof.
But intact will be the massive iron gates which limp from
their hinges and which are locked closed with a stout chain.
All of which says keep out. Take no special notice of any of
this. But continue on past the shiny leaved mass of
rhododendrons and wait till you encounter what looks like
an old rutted narrow overgrown boreen. Now this little
hedged in lane would have once been the exit from the
stately entrance drive you've already passed a wee bit back.
Such an arrangement being that in your old former grander

days one did not have to turn a vehicle around in front of the house but could with utter nonchalant convenience drive your carriages or motor car straight out another road. No small advantage to Your Nibs, the owner who can bloody well keep you, as you reverse all over the place, from rutting up his ruddy lawn. So if you've no mind of branches and briars scratching your car, go in this entrance. If it's day time you may be thinking you're entering a strange nightmare. Pay no attention to this overgrown jungle surprise. And fear not in the passing shadows the great writhing roots of the rhododendrons which would look like a bunch of hungry dark grey pythons ready to come and get you. St Patrick took care of all of them sorts of creatures. But hold on to your hat over the potholes. These would do more damage to you than cobras or crocodiles with your wheel axles breaking and mud splashing up into your gearbox. But take courage. Motor on. Worth it all for what you'll see at the end.

But first, before you reach the big house, hear a little more about your upper cruster man, His Nibs the pasha. In his worn and torn tweeds, his boots and cap and secluded beyond redemption in this grown wild estate, he would for a start have his gold cuff links holding his silk shirt cuffs together. And never mind the wintry rain pelting him, he'd be well adapted for his survival. He'd be late of a morning out of bed after his mountainous heap of bacon, eggs, tomatoes and sausages washed down with enough thick tea to float a battleship. He is, like the bastards who run yelping between his legs and around his house, born in Ireland. Indeed born up in the bedroom just below the very attic of the very mansion where he himself has put the scullery maids in calf. He has long been able to suffer both your descending and rising varieties of damp, which long ago seeped deep into your man's bones. While his labour force is out in the stableyard tackroom contemplatively having a smoke, he'd be wearing thick gloves and cap and still in his muddy boots as he sits huddled in front of his newspaper. His life is simplicity itself. He'd have long ago accepted the fact that no one but himself was going to be really attentive to minding his cattle. Or go as he does to open his own gates to his beef herd when it's thought time to let them graze further afield where the grass would be longer and sometimes even greener. And your men having a smoke in the tackroom would always be ready to drive the beasts into the yard for castration and skulling off their horns, the latter activity being their most highly enjoyed of farming chores. But soon your cattle themselves would be knowing this and by god before you had a chance to open a gate they'd put their own convenient holes in the hedge or fences and soon be gone distantly in a lot of your unwanted directions.

Now what has just happened is an event which brings about another of great significance. Lurking deep down in the soul of your pasha still glows an ember of imperialism and empire and the long learnt lessons taught that the natives should be kept in and know their place and such be demonstrated by all your outward signs of behaviour. And it is coincident with his final cattle escape that your man the squire finally throws down the gauntlet to admit and let it be known that he has gone unreservedly native. Availing as he does of the cheapest and fastest way of mending a broken fence or blocking up a gap in a hedge. For out of the big house and lugged down the servants' stairs come the old iron bed steads and springs from the many disused servants' rooms. And these often quite elaborately brass adorned furnishings are placed intertwined with a few briars or a stout bough of a blackthorn to hold them in the hedge gap or to block up a breached fence lashed with a strand or two of barbed wire. All of which fencing is utter anathema and blasphemy to your local fox hunting fraternity whose horses go crashing through such hedges and jumping over such fences. Which are now lethal flesh tearing obstacles to those pursuing the fox and which by god could leave you maimed and you and your horse broken necked. Needless to say, those galloping by booted, top hatted and well horsed, would regard you as being no longer of that highly acceptable ilk, the landed gentry, but instead would now see you as a country boor who has badly let the side down.

However, your presently eccentric squire gone native would still like when necessary to remain able to purchase your odd manmade necessity such as candles for the house, and so would soon need to sell an odd head or two of his unstrayed cattle at the market. And mind you he wouldn't have gone totally native in what he would do next. Taking a bath. Getting out a clean silk shirt. Popping in his best cuff links and with monocle gleaming over an eye, be taken by horse and carriage to the train to Dublin. Where, arriving in the metropolis, he would first deposit himself in the splendid ambience of the lounge of the Royal Hibernian Hotel or down in its buttery and quaff back a snipe of champagne. Letting himself get thoroughly bored before he would deign to escape from the noise and the people and go dine within the red brick sanctum of the Kildare Street Club. Followed later by much port and sport over an emerald glowing snooker table.

Meanwhile back at the farm, the mansion and the big estate, the downspouts are blocked and the dead leaves long settled and rotted in the roof gutters are causing drips descending the stone work. And some more of the slates have slipped. Leaving gaps that would have you dodging downpours within. And your man was long ago warned that the king post spanning his attic and holding aloft trusses and beams and which supported the surrounds of the glass dome that arches over the great entrance hall three storeys high, was weakened with rot. Now the theory is that, as everything has been this way for years past, why wouldn't it in the same mood of immobility last these few more years holding, as it has long held, the beams, trusses and rafters faithfully serving their purpose under the many tons of massive slates. And so it does in the ample timelessness available continue to miraculously do. Ah but them traitorous old prehistoric woodworms have since a past suddenly warm June been also wreaking their dusty havoc, and weakening the king post. And although this massive piece of timber is, outwardly at least, looking fine, within, it is but a crumbling brittle bit of old pulverulence that wouldn't hold up the weight of a monk's impure thought and would resemble more your morning piece of burnt toast that Bridget or Bridie have put blackened on your breakfast tray.

Now then. It is presently one fine day and your man His Nibs is out viewing and counting the cattle in a distant field. The sun is warm on the face. Your wrens chirping are flitting to and fro. Primroses and violets are glowing jewel like in yellow and purple and the shadows of the hedgerows. And suddenly your man hears what he thinks is a clap of thunder. Now I can tell you here and now it's not. Your man takes off his cap and scratches his head in wonderment for there's not a trace of a storm or a cloud this day in the length and breadth of the sky. He goes about his business. Strolling to the lake where the swans glide. Walking over the soft turf. The day is like any other. But when he returns and climbs the front steps of the big house and opens the great oak door into his entrance hall he trips over a plaster cornice in smithereens. He takes off his cap and looks up. The roof beams are hanging askew, just as further remnants of plaster plummet down to hit him in his left, monocled eye. And upon this utterly clement, peaceful day he knows the fatal moment has come.

Now don't for a moment feel sorry for him. Feel sorry for the ruddy upper floors of the house. Wasn't your man already this long time of an evening having his meals down in the cellar kitchen by the stove and there munching a few chunks of beef taken from his big bowl of hot potatoes while last week's socks hung drying over the hot water pipes. The remaining retainers in the farm force, Sean, Paddy and Mick, would be out by the stove in the tack-room, caps still on in the Irish tradition while you eat, and themselves also comfortably digging into the boiled spuds with them floating in a bit of milk made golden with a great gob of melted butter. Now shielded by the kitchen ceiling from your immediate inclemencies, and while having a decent meal, your man is thinking it over that an entrance hall wasn't that vital. Sure anytime he liked he could enter the generous sized door that led in from the stable yard. And in any event since his conversation had got distinctly monosyllabic and was now consisting mostly of abrupt grunts, and the damp had long ago stuck all his visiting cards together, hardly a soul was recently coming to call upon him. And certainly no talkative Americans would dare, in fear of continued disappearance, approach up his lane. Plus seeing that there was now your actual grass growing up out of his cap and a spare blade or two actually to be seen coming out from behind his left ear. Always a sure sign to any one of his fellow Protestant worshippers standing behind him in chapel that he'd finally gone totally, absolutely, homegrown indigenous. With his double barrelled surname the only alien British thing about him left. And for those people whose clipped vowels are still cutting rapier sharp through the Celtic air and whose destinations are Ascot, Henley and Wimbledon come June and whose drawing room drink is gin and tonic, this is very much an off putting sight in one regarded previously as of their ilk.

Everybody now all over the parish and beyond has heard what has happened to your man's king post. And you'd think that the time had come for His Nibs, of the grassy ear and the fallen down entrance hall, to be putting his mind to salvaging at least in a financial way what he could from the disaster. And be dancing about inviting the more aggressive of your antique dealers to rush in where his previous friends of the ascendancy now gravely fear to tread. But not a bit of it. The front gate that you passed previously has had its big chain twice more wrapped around its rungs and is padlocked. And there's not a trace of a sign of an antique dealer in his gent's natty suiting making offers to your man room by room for the objets d'art, the gilt mirrors, the plethora of console tables, the early George III giltwood mirrors, the Regency sidetables, not to mention the candelabra, silverware, and porcelain and delphware from all kinds of distant dynasties and them bunch of old bound volumes you've got there unread packing the walls and taking up the space in that big library.

The truth of the matter is, your delapsing man in your delapsing mansion was no materialist. And never was. And them Georgian gilt mirrors reflecting the rest of the now dusty, damp furnishings and hanging still resplendent all over the brocade walls and adorning above the mantel pieces of this great house, will meet another and different fate. Which is to be left right where they are. For your usually mild mannered man would take a shotgun to you should anything of this gracefully decaying past be disturbed in this house. Yet to the non pushy predator wandering near just to have a peek, if he did not ask you later to have a cup of tea, he would at least invite you to go in. And to use the servant's entrance from the stableyard and warn you of the falling masonry, ceiling plaster, rotted floors and roof beams. But at least you'd get a chance to peruse this once grand place before it would all crumble to join, as His Nibs would, the soil again.

But now he himself, before he got bopped in the skull with a falling joist, has moved into a groom's quarters in the stableyard where your simple comforts were still to be had with the plain panelled walls upon which tack and saddles hang. A cot and a few wool blankets. A nice little wood stove in the middle of the room. Ah but back in the big house, your man's coat and cap, untouched collecting dust these many months, are still left hanging in the corridor leading off to the grand entrance hall. The main staircase impassable upwards is now in a state of collapse so you would have no trouble coming down it pretty fast. One now gains entrance to the upper floors by a servants' back stairs. For unbelievably a hardy Bridget and Bridie are still hanging out in the drier parts of their attic quarters where above their heads remain a few of the slates intact on the roof. For they'd rather not live out in a horse box in the stableyard, and with nowhere else to go, they will finally go down with this sinking ship. But as you'd imagine in a religious humane country like Ireland a contingent of nuns from the convent in the nearby town finally came out to rescue them.

The meadows and parklands are still out there stretching as they always did to the plantation of trees on the horizon. But even here too one can see the dilapidations as the boughs of branches broken from the ancient oaks form their contorted shapes on the land and the cattle come to trample the turf to mud as they stand scratching and rubbing on the splintered sharp tips of the fallen timber. The pot holes in the exit drive, are now great ruts which can wrench a wheel from a vehicle. The front gates strain on the chain locking them as they teeter further over. The gate lodge with the tree growing through its roof now has its doors torn off and windows broken by passing vandals. And back at the big house a dissonant strain of music is heard reverberating. It is nearly the last chord to be ever sounded on the concert grand piano in the drawing room. For the weight of the large Regency giltwood and verre églomise over-mantel mirror aseat on the chimney piece has finally loosened itself from its moorings in the wall and has crashed face down on the keyboard. And in so doing has also knocked over a pair of George III ormolu and white marble king's vase candelabra which go toppling to crash upon the flower decorated silk Heriz rug. And never mind what it did to the delicate gilt leaves and ornament of the Louis XVI white marble and ormolu astronomical mantel timepiece now stopped ticking for all time. Plus at that same exact moment too, unquestionably in sympathy, a group of late eighteenth century lock pistols chose to fall from where they have been long mounted on the brocaded wall. And let me tell you, with the little people the fairies loose and running all over this tumbling down house and now upending everything in sight as they usually do, it becomes no place where any serious connoisseur collector of your better antiques could avoid feeling sick to his stomach before he has his apoplectically hysterical heart attack. And as time marches on and in his same mood of neutrality your man His Nibs is out in the stable yard in his little cosy groom's cottage, a bit of old cabbage boiling with the potatoes in the black iron pot suspended over the embers of the turf fire, his boots off, legs stretched out and his feet propped up on a log while the damp evaporates from his socks with an anciently sweaty fume. And caring not a damn that another chord reaches his ears as another section of the ceiling plasterwork plummets on to the concert grand piano's ivory keys.

Ah now I know what you're thinking, you are thinking such falling down places with an occupant such as Your Nibs in it are the extreme exception rather than the usual rule and are not to be found up at the rutted end of every overgrown boreen all over the country. Instead you'd be thinking that your overwhelmed descending member of the Anglo Irish ascendancy would be removing the slates and lead off the roof, the chimney pieces out of the rooms, the chandeliers off the ceilings and, along with the furnishing contents, filling up the backs of lorries and whipping them into the antique dealers and auction emporiums to flog them for every penny they can get. And you'd be right.

And this sort would with the proceeds, build themselves a bijou bungalow to which their entrance drive would conspicuously lead. And in which, at the cocktail hour, they would serve their gin drinks. And invite friends like themselves to play bridge on Thursdays. And there'd be no Bridget, Bridie and Dymphna left there lurking in the attics, polishing, cleaning, cooking and scrubbing and who would have to be later rescued by the nuns. But instead ensconced, and adding to the bungalow blight, are these unsentimental uninspired folk desirous of their daily little comforts. Who would strip Ireland of her treasures, and peddle these to the commercially marauding stranger.

Ah but we're not quite finished yet with the annals of the big country house. There'd be your other type and variety of persons who have found a method of keeping roofs on, walls from falling and your objets d'art and antique furnishings and paintings intact as well as keeping even better than potatoes, broccoli and Brussels sprouts steaming on their plates. These hombres and women folk have come to curious terms with not only the preservation of the family seat but with the neat trick of themselves remaining seated more than ever decently comfortably in it. What they do is to sell these vast houses and their parklands to your foreigner. And then by god under codicil make the arrangement with the new owner to remain therein put, as your cook and butler, descended now into the basement to take up their servants' duties. Now then, the new and generally highly charming owner has for a good long stretch of time each year to be back in his native country making the big decisions which make the money to provide upkeep for his newly acquired pile. And upon each such departure of the new owner to attend to his business, the

previous occupants of the stately manse take off their servants' uniforms, remove from their damp quarters in the
basement and plant themselves right back up in their previous, and much drier upstairs apartments. Once again
residing in their former grandness and strutting about in
jodhpurs and cravats, they immediately get a Bridget and
Dymphna out from the town to do this and do that and
don't forget to genuflect. Indeed you'll never see anything
like it the way they now throw their weight about and get
not a little bit stroppy with the outside staff, plus issue
invitations to all their old gentry pals to come dine on the
wine cellar and kitchen largesse of the presently absentee
landlord.

Now this switch from master to servant and back again
from servant to master, convenient as the arrangement may
be for both parties, does not always operate without your
occasional grievously and often fatal embarrassing incident.
I mean to say, here you have your Frenchman, Italian, German or immensely rich Spaniard flying back to Ireland from
your hectic board meetings in Paris, Rome, Frankfurt or
Madrid and ready to collapse for a deep long soak in a hot
bath far from the stresses of these busy European cities.
And ruddy bloody hell, would you believe it, your butler
and cook just removed back to below stairs have used up
every ounce of the hot water for their own leisurely baths.
Plus while you were this time lengthy away have also
depleted the wine cellar of your very best burgundy, vintage champagne and Napoleon brandy. But worse and much
worse even than the inclemencies presently raging outside
your shuttered dining room, is that your butler and cook
down in the basement have just following your return and
the arrival of your glamorously chic guests from Paris, been

getting tipsy in an Irish manner you would not believe. Of course as might be expected in your high powered way of life, you've invited your very top drawer haute couture designers, industrial magnates, and jet setting social luminaries to get away from it all in each other's scintillating company and luxuriate in your sprawling thirty two bedroom mansion this weekend. At least the candles are already lit in the dining room and the smoky fire has been got to ignite by exercising your lungs blowing on it. And now you hear your butler and cook Stephen and Gretchen both approaching with the victuals along the long dark corridor where by god they do, within your hearing, be letting off a loud bit of steam. And there you all sit famished in your finery and transplanted from Paris, waiting for the food and you as host being dismissive about your acquiring such a grand house so ruddy bloody cheaply. Which your guests have no trouble believing as they await already shivering out of their wits with teeth chattering from the ice cold baths they are too embarrassed to say they have, like you also, just attempted. But such physical discomfort is nothing compared to the social discomfort which is about to befall. Your erstwhile Gretchen and Stephen, respectively Gretch and Steve as they are now called and formerly lord and lady of the manor are raising their voices in the hall. The vein of such shouting being to do with caste and class. Especially their social class and their previous entitlements and your social class and your present assumed presumptions as the new incumbent. You may not hear words like impostor, nouveau riche, upstart and parvenue. But by god you will hear these former country house owners spouting off as to how grand they once were at their London débutante balls, and local fox hunting shindigs and how certainly even in their socially reduced circumstances, remained a lot grander than the folk to whom they now had the demeaned duty of presently lugging and serving the spuds and artichokes brought over from Paris out of season. Of course old Steve, as your butler, is the distinct lesser of this evening's evil for he has been, as a long time lush, happily down the cellars sampling the plethora of wines and cigars from early afternoon and only interrupted when he took a bottle of champagne up to quaff in his bath. And following which he then repaired to the front east drawing room in his satin bathrobe to, glass in hand, beseat himself on your George III giltwood open armchair, sampling a dram or two of your armagnac as he mildly regrets the price at which he sold you the objets d'art he formerly owned. Now don't forget that old Gretch the wife now the cook in the kitchen is only just a short way along the basement corridor from the wine cellar and has been constantly repairing there for the rum, sherry and whiskey she requires added to the various dishes she's been exotically concocting. And of course she too takes a sampling swalick from her bevy of bottles all now standing nearly empty and hidden under draped dishtowels. Nor forget that these former owner occupiers have enduringly hard stomachs and throats. And there they now stand the pair of them mortally fractured out of their minds at the pantry door and totally smashed senseless with the eyes in their heads revolving like celestial globes of no particular description as they make their swaying efforts to balance the cauldrons of soup and stew they each bear.

Of course any foreigner attracted to Ireland for any length of time would be a person of some pleasant sensitivity and tolerance but now you as the new pasha sit with your mouth open in both hunger and horror as your guests, aghast, reach for their napkins. And you wait till it is the very last second before you jump up in your effort to stop old Steve from pitching forward crashing with his tureen of soup splashing in every direction over the dining room floor. Not that any of this awful stuff, into which old Gretch has mistakenly dumped a jar of marmalade and two bottles of ketchup, is going to taste any good anyway. However, old Gretch as she now loses her balance, makes a grab for Steve's arms and drops her own armful of drunkenly prepared ingredients. While her husband, suddenly yanked forward, trips and sends flying the soup splattering over the dining room table. And your folk from Paris, although saved from having to sample this stodgy emulsion, find that their napkins held over their evening wear are no protection from this wave of bright beet-coloured liquid. And they now witness poor old Steve upon his hands and knees crawling through Gretchen's stew to escape between some lady's knees under the dining room table. Lesson enough that your Anglo Irish landed gentry in trying their hand at a little cooking and butlering revert to being as fecklessly inept as Bridget, Bridie and Dymphna ever were and simply have not got their hearts in it in ministering to their masters.

Ah but now as the modern Ireland emerges where everything or anything is for sale or rent, there is yet another ilk of your great country house inhabitant who not only are still around and continuing to own their stately piles but who are even rubbing a few coins together. These sophisticates of your gentry folk are possessed surprisingly of a certain business expertise. And they simply advertise in your stylish glossy magazines abroad. Either renting out for the seasons of fishing, shooting or fox hunting, or for a stretch of the warmer summer months. Retaining a most favoured room or two, the country house owner locks up his private papers and either moves to Spain or to a not too distant outhouse on the estate. From where, sad to say, the owner's wife with high powered binoculars peers with resentment at the paying intruder having the solitary pleasure of her pleasure gardens. And it is not always some rich fat old chocolate munching battleaxe from your Park Avenue in New York who is out of a morning on the garden paths ignoring the roses. But often one finds a genial and kindly old lady glad of the space and the grand dignity of moving among gleaming antiques and ancestral portraits. And at the prices charged, who could resent such a dear. But alas, more times it is your face lifted hard bitten bitch who is out sneering at your weeds bursting up all over the pleasure gardens or at the algae green stale water in the ice cold outdoor swimming pool. And of course indoors she is shouting for service from the household staff who are hiding quietly out of sight in the most distant bedrooms.

But in spite of the vast rent you're charging and that they're willingly paying, there is a delicate point here. No matter who it is of these persons you have rented to, it does do something irking to you to have strangers sleeping between your coronet embroidered linen sheets and sitting upon your flower decorated porcelain crapper. And then bathing with your imported from Paris bath salts in your private sensuously delightful ancient copper bathtub the sensation of which you have so long cherished. But the Irish of whatever social persuasion have never lost their faith in the eternal affluence of the foreigner. And these visiting folk are not only just rich, rich, rich. They are bloody damn rich, rich, rich. And it is to this land long renowned for its poverty that these well heeled now stream in their thousands. They arrive in Ireland with their secretaries in tow, their limousines with chauffeur having been flown in ahead of time to meet them. And how could they ever be called gaudy or inelegant wanting as they so genuinely do to sample the indoor aristocratic ambience of the life lived by these European gentry in their great noble country houses as their ancestors have done going back the hundreds of years. And wanting to flex your self importance kitted out in gown and black tie, and then reflected in the mirror on your grand staircase landing, descend slowly step by step purring with conceit to attend upon dinner. Where god forbid that the previous Gretch and Steve should be lurking in wait to dance their brand of attendance upon you.

You may have now so far gathered that Ireland is a tourist trap, albeit of some unique qualities. Especially if your physical and particularly your financial capabilities allow you to pursue the country house routine of fox hunting, shooting and fishing. For there still are a few unspoilt miles left of land, lake and river. Plus let me tell you that in Ireland the first unmistakably genuine thing you sample is the bloody damp chill. Which even in summer amid these three foot thick stone walls of the mansion you're renting can freeze the tits off even your best upholstered ladies. And if her husband is not dead yet, and travelling with her, can make his balls clatter ice stricken together till they bust in small smithereens. And in addition, as he tries to brush his teeth with them chattering in his head of a morning, the amount of toothpaste he swallows ruins his appetite for breakfast. But cheer up. As each year goes by much more central heating and soft toilet tissue will have come.

But surely, you're suggesting, there is yet another way that your native home grown squire holds on to his stately home and estate. And by golly yes there is. And although it takes a bit of your more intimate elbow rubbing it's got its recompense. Your previous pasha squire who has solicited in your stylishly glossy, better foreign and American periodicals now lets it be known he is ready for a paying guest or two. Who might enjoy taking up residence for a few days and will wine and dine right in the company of one who is to the manner and manor born, and be safely permitted to ramble freely around his estate. Of course all these visiting folk are courteously warned to come with their dinner jackets, ball gowns and sweaters packed. The main big feature being the nightly intimate dinner parties with the lord and lady of the house. Who, although they will not join you for tea after your bags are unpacked, will nevertheless see you get real hot from the oven scones and a bowl of clotted cream with your choice of morello cherry, strawberry or blueberry jam. And this time honoured and nearly sacred ritual in front of your blazing library fire will really knock you out. And alert you to the plenty of more pleasures to come.

Now you may have suffered in your considerable accumulation of worldly riches, many a snub due to your generally disagreeable looks, or worse, sneers at your race, creed or colour. So if you are unhandsome in appearance or a member in good standing of a reviled and thoroughly dis- liked and resented minority, the one thing you are really going to find an absolute delight here and totally contrary to what the world has been led to believe about this isle, is the utter lack of ethnic and religious prejudice. Nor is there any reason in the least to feel inferior in the atmosphere created by your host's voice. Which will in this unusually sophisticated gentleman be of a most highly polished elegance. Which at the outset might delude you into thinking that you are in for a stuffy stay. Far from it. Your squire will put on a show you won't forget. Indeed verging on the vaudevillian, this aristocratic and eccentric member of the gentry will be found to be a startling revelation altogether and unlikely to be encountered ever again anywhere. So make the most of him. Listen to his every broad minded, unbigoted plain spoken word. Watch him enjoy with gusto his Sancerre and salmon mousse as he sits up at his presiding end of the table in his blue velvet smoking jacket and in a damn good mood since you are paying quite an astonishing whack for your bed, breakfast and nightly dinner. And note too that there is nothing mediocre about the wine, and the food you and he are presently devouring is plentiful and delicious. Although he doesn't mind your suspect table manners in sipping from the finger bowl or your reaching for the wrong spoon or in your asking him how far back his lineage really goes. Or should you be that crass to ask if that enormous pedigree hanging in the front hall is actually all his. Nor does he mind in the least if you question the solid quality of the vastly tall heavy candelabra softly glowing the pleasant light all over the dining room. So sit back and enjoy the utter genuineness of everything and everyone around you. You may bet your last two dollars that his ancestry goes back so distantly far that you are nearly dealing with the zoological origin of the species. And that the family tree elaborated in its four colour variation out in the front hall is only part of what he could display of warrants, patents, birthrights and titles. And you can depend too that the every inch and ounce of the silverware in this stately home is sterlingly substantial as is the gold your twenty four carat quality. And suddenly right in the middle of all your indiscreet questioning your host will tweak the end tips of his black bow tie, fetch out his monocle tucked in his cummerbund and place it deeply in his eye. And only a moment of silence precedes his launching into his best version of his stage Irish accent in all its mellifluous peasant colouration. And this is, as he in an instant switches from his usual culturally pure Oxonian Queen's English, a phonetic treat without parallel to behold. For amid his jolly ranting, little particles of food, usually associated with the lower orders, will realistically fly from his lips. Of course he will readily admit to perhaps an ancestral indiscretion allowing an occasional peasant interloper to infiltrate his lineage. And will often at this point, as his pièce de resistance, get up, and while pulling his forelock, dance around the dining room like a clod hopping, bog trotting potato digger. Although his elegant and beautiful wife may not show unbridled enthusiasm for these antics you yourself may well find that you are being splashed as you uncontrollably guffaw into your soup.

Of course, as you might expect, there are your slightly more serious snags in staying as a paying guest in some of these country houses. Your hostess herself sometimes would really rather you weren't around at all, and occasionally has difficulty in disguising it, especially as having already impressed you and made you feel as inferior to her as invariably you actually are, due, of course, to parental consequences beyond your control. Also, instead of haughtily lofty service in the manner of a genuine liveried footman bringing around the bowls of Brussels sprouts and steaming spuds, some of your stately hosts adopt what you might regard as a boarding house routine when you find yourself blatantly handed in plain style your plate already covered with its servings of food. Don't mind this one little bit. Look at it in the honest homey plentiful manner in which it is meant. And fork up what you fancy of this usually generally tasty home grown and nutritious fare. Your host without coaxing will further regale you with his brogue and may even, when he's feeling exceptionally chipper, sing an Irish ballad to prolong the collective happy atmosphere. But do prepare yourself not to take amiss his outspoken rudeness about the people, behaviour and places in the country you hale from. Remembering always that your man the host, widely travelled and sophisticated as he is, is your real eccentric in a land full of eccentrics, and this is just a friendly little exercise to encourage you and your kinsmen to keep yourselves up to scratch. Something he himself is not averse to doing in calling, say, a local hotel to order, and not mincing his words when he designates the place a prize shit hole to the proprietor's face.

But hold on. You may at this point as a paying guest, pat yourself on the back and take a little credit here. Your evening in this country house is waning and mellowness has settled upon your chaps as the port has for the third time passed around during the telling of generally uproarious bawdily indiscreet stories and the ladies who have withdrawn are now to be joined by the gentlemen. You are by your mere presence helping your host to defray the cost, and in effect contributing to save the remaining handful of these great houses, castles and grand mansions. Encouraging them to still stand and remain able to function with their sadly depleted staffs, which at least keeps the ivy vines from clinging and climbing the stone walls and creeping into their master's bedroom windows, finally to entwine around his four poster bed. For while these gentry folk stay alive and kicking under their top hats and tiaras, and their smiles keep smiling from glossy social magazines, it is their voices alone which are raised to embarrass, to shame, if not stop, the gombeen marauder. They alone prevent the stripping of the big slates, roof lead, and keep the doric columns from falling. They alone prevent a night's pale moonlight from finally shining through this stately mansion's front open door through which the winds might blow and upon whose front hall floor might gather a soft blanket of leaves. They alone preserve from the mould of death just one more edifice of the many already crumbled back into the landscape, and which was once part of Ireland and whose existence can boast of its being wrought there by Irish hands.

And
Thank your lucky
Eccentric stars
Who save
These stones
From further tumbling
Down.

JUST AS THE KNOTS ARE WELL TIED HOLDING THE

WEIGHT OF THIS STONE TO KEEP HAY FROM

STRAYING IN THE WIND, SO IS AN IRISHMAN'S

BODY STILL BUILT FOR WORK AND CAUTION FOR

THE FUTURE STILL WRIT UPON HIS FACE.

IV

But let us get back to your ordinary sort of down to earth Irishman, who by god in his own way and through an occasional fault of his own, has helped keep intact this country's widespread Irish reputation. For there is yet another type whom you might at first glance think is an arriviste interloper. But you would be grievously wrong. For your man, despite his present day appearance in his gent's natty suiting, was here once before, being born and raised on this landscape and would, prior to the advent of television, have been doing his bit of forelock pulling. But now, let me tell you, he would deign to take up the role of squire and move in where your previous Anglo Irish tread as settler landlords. He would appear out of the utter blue from your distant continents of Australia, America or even the next parish of Britain itself. This successful nouveau riche gentleman would be stepping down out of your first class compartment of your boat or aeroplane and he and the wife be festooned with the latest in luggage in which is packed their jade pot to piss in. Your man, all smiles, also would, if it wasn't so filthy with litter, even kiss the ground he arrives on. But instead bursting at the seams with his packs of punt notes, the well known playful native currency, he boards his limousine. Get ready for him. For the Big man would be coming at you like a steam locomotive loose on the tracks. His good intention being that now back home he'd show them a thing or two about being high and mighty as would make even your former gentry take notice. Rolling as he now does down the laneways in his conspicuously élitist monstrous long vehicle with your plethora of mink rugs, shooting sticks, pairs of binoculars strewn everywhere over the back seats. And if, stopping at the pub, they were stolen while he was in having a drink he'd only nod assent and say to those avidly witnessing and listening around him,

"Ah now me boyos there'd be more of them same things as have gone missing to be got where they came from."

Now then. Plain sailing is never your general condition in Ireland. And there'd be too, a few of your other difficulties maybe not counted on by your Big man. The next of these being the width of the big car that won't fit to go down the old boreen, up and down which he ran barefoot to collect the milk and drive cattle as a child. And where at the muddy end of it he would now deign to roll up in his limo at the front door to be visiting his relatives in style. Plus having already had most of the vehicle's contents stolen from outside the pub, he'd be a little less anxious to have it left now up on the main road. Even if it was suitably surrounded by the neighbours hoping to have an envious peek in the windows at the finery. But never mind, he's now bought the big house beyond with the great ballroom and with the wide big gates where there'd be no similar trouble of space for his limousine to squeeze between the vegetation. And with him now able to roar in the gateway over the apron of pebbles and up the mile long drive to this grand great mansion once occupied by your previous Anglo Irish gentry. And why wouldn't he smile passing between the rolling parklands to take up residence in this edifice long dominating the landscape and which he's bought cheap at the price.

Now your mansion into which your Big man has moved consists of four storeys high over a basement and with eleven bays on its front elevation. And having unforgivingly sat these past three years empty and unattended it would, as the estate agent said, be in need of a few of your renovations and repairs. But sure, a lick of paint here, a joist mended there and a few of your chimneys rebuilt and slates replaced, and bob is your rud. This last expression often used by estate agents to denote that everything is to be finally gained by buying this house and that the extensive dilapidations shouldn't trouble you since money is no object and you can with an army of builders put the place back in good nick in no more time than would take a few years. Optimism is the theme song here. And this returned, flush with quids Irishman wanting plenty of freedom and space for himself, the wife and kiddies plus the few horses he would be keeping, has also bought the extensive acreage surrounding this mansion. For real wealth to the Irishman is land. And this land is land the agent has represented as being in good heart and your man should be glad of every acre he could get. And with a few cattle grazing it would keep it that way. And as sure as bob is still your rud, all you have to do is open up a gate betimes to let them in and out. The rest you leave to them ripping off their mouthfuls of grass and putting on the pounds, shillings and pence while you have a late hot bath of a morning.

Now although your Big man wasn't born yesterday he'd listen calmly enough to your estate agent extolling the money making virtue of cattle. And not many weeks later he'd have your pedigree herd out on the parklands and already have got your teams of builders in to put the missing slates back on the roof, rebuild the chimneys, and screw in tight again the hinges of the limping shutters. Action everywhere as the roof gutters are cleaned and the downspouts are rid of blockages and the dry rot poison is pumped in the walls. Ah but the native workforce has different ideas of decorating, architecture, plumbing and electricity than they do in the distant places where your Big man made all his money, and with plenty of your best advice at his elbow which he always had the good sense to follow. But already he is out of breath rushing to the crisis sites where the eager to please workforce had torn the faded threadbare silk wall coverings from the main reception rooms, and had already pasted on your latest brocaded orange striped maroon ersatz wallpaper. Ah but with the hammers still banging and wrenches still clanging, the misunderstandings upstairs, bad as they are, are nothing like those as has been going on down in the damp dungeons of your cellars where the gang of them are now non plussed scratching their heads over the big rusty pipes left there from the last hopeless attempt made by the occupying gentry to heat this massive house. And now your plumbers availing of the convenience of the previous pipes, have lost track of their own guaranteed hot central heating arrangements they'd mapped out to rage the calorifics through the miles of pipes in this mansion. With the moment now reached when the system has to be switched on for its trial testing. With hands resting on the radiators just to find out where water would, by a miracle, bring a little warmth. The switch has been thrown. The oil booms into flames in the furnace. The circulating pump surges the water through the pipes. And by god folks, get ready with your boots, oilskins and umbrella. For coming pouring at you through your brand new wallpapers just pasted up in every blessed room of the house, are your streaming jets of rusty liquid staining and soaking every blessed thing in sight. Let me tell you your Big man didn't half do an Irish jig on the ballroom centre of the parquet floor.

Now normally you'd need an ambulance in a hurry for the apoplexy but fortunately we're not dealing with an American here whose countrymen, in similar Irish circumstances, have been known to enter into hair tearingly permanent nervous breakdowns. But never mind such plumbing drawbacks for the moment. For by god your Big man has put in the nearby town's local newspaper adverts for servants of your reliable teetotal non smoking domestic variety. And now even as this house stands unfinished and is damp and icily cold, a butler, a cook, three maids and a gardener plus three men for the farm are on their way to make themselves immediately available to dance attendance upon this returned Irishman and his family. Who has just provided each of his five kids with his or her own pony. Now if you think waterfalls coming out of your random walls through leaks in the central heating pipes and pouring down through floor boards were giving your man a touch of exasperation, you have no knowledge then of the local willing and ready Irish domestic servant. For these be now in this day and age of a calibre that would, if you were serious in your enjoyment of life, be best to avoid and forget. Yet the optimism attached in assuming the mantle of squire, is possessed of a certain momentum and becomes an irrepressible disease as the disasters accumulate. With your returned rich Irishman stubbornly laying down the household law as your domestic servants just as stubbornly flaunt it while ensconced as they are, solid as you please, in your big mansion where they await over their cups of tea their Friday's wage packets. Of course your Big man is not having too much of that, and doesn't he pull on the switch to the central heating to jolt them out of their kitchen complacency with a wall and ceiling burst of water jets from the faulty plumbing pipes.

Now you'd think that your local populace, who live in the parish surrounding the big house and who summer evenings convene at the nearby crossroads to make gossip and conduct a bit of courtship, would be dancing and clapping their hands with triumphal joy now that one of their own had taken over and supplanted the ascendant invader. Well you'd be woefully, blatantly and unmistakably wrong. Sure, like when your man's car was parked outside the pub with the binoculars and mink rugs gone missing, they'd be now only trying to borrow a tool or two that would never be seen again. And don't accuse them of polite stealing. Sure didn't they bring it back a week ago and if it's gone again now it would be through no fault of theirs. So here you have your staffed household who have overnight, by a turn of phrase, become butlers, cooks, maids and gardeners. And experts, all of them at drinking tea while polishing the chairs with their backs and arses for comfort, or if dispatched to dig up a spud or two in the garden, are leaning upon their forks in either rain or sunshine. Sure why should they aid and abet people no better than themselves to be putting on airs up in the big house, sitting mightily as you please on swansdown cushions, mixing their tea with silver spoons and with candlelight no less from the candelabra casting shadows over their steaming plates. And by god the butler himself, who wouldn't know a George III ormolu mounted yew wood and marquetry commode from the back of his foot, or a burgundy from a Chateau d'Yquem, is here now pretending elaborate ceremony in pouring out your choice of red or white wine to wash down the boiled bacon, potatoes and cabbage.

However, your returned Irishman with the plethora of quids now up in the mansion didn't make his money out of nothing. He'd have already raged flying around the house trying to get at the pipes with a wrench to seal them off. But then would find instead it made much more sense to chase the plumber out and down the front drive and as far away as possible. However, there is also a thing too, lately come to Ireland, called electricity and someone called an electrician who would have in a similar fashion to your self taught plumbers been installing your wires instead of your pipes. And which has not only produced your rusty rainfall and widespread flooding but has also now added the distinct hazard of possible death by electrocution. Your Big man finding that when he presses to switch on a light in the water closet a light instead goes on in the kitchen below and he's left peeing over his foot in the darkness. And to turn on a light in his bedroom he's found he has to distantly go out in the stable yard. And to turn out the stable yard light he has to return to his bedroom. But talking about electric light and its recent introduction into the mansion, your Big man would at least have the shrewd suspicion and enough presence of mind at night not only to have the shutters closed but the curtains drawn so as not to give the more inquisitive of the local population creeping up under the cover of darkness the opportunity to snicker and laugh peeking in the night time windows at some of their own in black tie. And especially with the ladies sporting voluminously flowing gowns with their necklines daringly deeply plunging while pushing their silver forks between their dentures. And by god you'd wake up soon to something you didn't think was rampant here in Ireland and that be the sudden turbulent rising up and plunging down of social class.

But back in your mansion kitchen your man the self taught butler originally from County Monaghan, and who in fact did at least work long enough to get fired from his last three jobs in England for being falling down drunk in charge of three respective wine cellars. And now semi-retired and, as it happens, back again out in the bogs, is busy enough once more with the bottles. Opening them left, right and centre and tasting the contents. But he'd only be wanting to make sure the wine hadn't turned into vinegar and that the vintage whiskey wasn't past its peak. And he'd have to hurry as there were plenty of bottles to sample yet. So it would not be long now till your man the butler was having difficulty finding his way from pantry to dining room, having crashed back down the cellar stairs and taken a sizeable knock on the head. And as a result, and now also needing to desperately relieve himself after all the liquid intake, was now opening the wrong doors to the wrong hallways. Finally, as his ill luck would have it and thinking he'd found the water closet door and having already in anticipation opened his fly and taken out his member, he was standing confronting the dinner guests inside the dining room chamber and distinctly without a pot in sight to piss in, and unable to control himself any longer, your butler's urine is landing in every hysterical direction around him. With female screams now coming from the pantry, and the ladies jumping up from their dining chairs and your man the butler non plussed as to the protocol to be assumed in the situation.

Now the butler wasn't all that great a sober sight to look at in the first place before all this present pother drunkenly happened. But at least he had enough good manners, seeing as to where he was relieving himself, to turn as soon as he could to rush back out the door. But also as Celtic luck would have it at this precise moment, high faluting guests, remnants of castle occupying Anglo Irish aristocracy, who have been invited, are late just arriving in their evening finery, and trying to find their way to their hosts, instead find themselves plunged into darkness as someone or something has just shorted the lights of the mansion. Now these eccentric folk who, although members of the lofty aristocracy, would still be on your best terms with your high and mighty powers and politicians in the government. So your Big man would be beside himself to please them and continue to enjoy planning permissions and other big favours that might come his way. And of course right now they have been stumbling lost on their way to the dining room. Where in the very best embarrassing manner these politically sensitive folk are suddenly run straight into in the bleakest of hall darkness by the butler trying to return his appendage to the privacy of his buttoned up trousers. Well let me tell you, between the cries of women in distress from the dining room, and the butler frontally charging at them in the hallway which naturally puts your Anglos into a panic, it's no wonder it richly results in a knock down drag out battle with no one knowing whose hair is being removed by the roots or who is punching them. The most terrible part of which is that here in the house of the Big man, as he comes out to investigate by candlelight, his butler is, while in an exposed state, busy belting the bejesus out of his guests of honour, who are already making a beeline as best they can tripping over the furniture towards the front door, and down the steps and into their Daimler car to roar away. And they are the lucky and prudent ones. But perhaps in this traditionally sentimental land they are not the most spirited or most understanding. For your Big man now in the blaze of the candelabra brought out from the dining room, helps your chap the butler up off the floor, brushes him down, waits patiently while the exposed private is returned to the privacy of your house steward's trousers. Then your Big man sits him on a chair and gives him a sup of brandy to revive his optimism. And one thing you would know by the conversation that follows would be that you could be no place else but in the Singular Country of Ireland.

"Ah sir, thanks be to god for the bit of brandy. And now I'm awfully sorry for that little bit of mistaken identity both with the water closet and your just arriving guests I thought were some brazen interlopers out from town. I hope that the inconvenient and unintentional relieving of myself and the inhospitality shown your two persons just departed will leave no lasting ill effects or feelings."

A SINGULAR COUNTRY

"Ah Paddy now me oul fella, drink up your brandy now. There'd be more folk available like them where they come from. And isn't piss good for carpets and sure if it soaks through them will be killing the dry rot rampant in the dining room floor. And don't be worrying as to them who have gone without staying to have the courtesy to enquire as to the clear mistake as must have been made. Let it be good riddance to them."

And here now
Straighten out your throat
And
Have another sup
Of brandy.

IN THE MILD AIR AND SINGULAR SILENCE OF THIS

KERRY LAND THE MYSTIQUE OF THE WEST IS HERE

GREATEST AWAKE WHICH DOTH BETIMES MAKE

THE SOUL SHIVER.

V

Ah but in Ireland, a land where shoplifters declared unfair police scrutiny in their first national strike, it is not always your man the butler, a bottle to his lips, and with piss drenched trouser cuffs who deliberately or accidentally stirs up the major mayhem. Or with wandering fingers interferes up the dresses of the female scullery help and then, summoned to duty, totters to crash face first into the giant tureen of soup he was on the way to ferry into the array of prominent guests waiting famished to dine as midnight approached. It would far more often be the entire lot of your Big man's household staff who would, by first going bolshi, refuse to attend to duties in any guise whatsoever. Requiring your returned nouveau riche Irishman to go with raised fists shouting to play pop backstage in the kitchens and pantry and search aloft in the floors and reassembling the staff he would by candlelight blandishment see to it that the dinner party is underway once more and attendance being danced upon his very important political guests.

And it is appropriate here to have a word about this last mentioned above category of person. For much is at stake to make a decent impression on the powers that be in Irish politics. And present at your Big man's table in the mansion might be your mightiest men in the nation. And they are on the whole basically a modest lot and not given to pretensions. Indeed so down to earth are some of them you might be forgiven for being utterly taken aback. Of rural, farming or publican background, they are for the most part bluff, gregarious, happy-to-see-you folk and always glad to present themselves at a decent hooley. Nor would they ever be averse to spending a few minutes of their valuable time with some old lady up an overgrown boreen, taking tea in the humblest of hovels. For eyes are watching them on every side. And by god do they know it. And for this reason do most recently arrive in the more conspicuous helicopter that you'd see coming noisily over the hills at you, or for those afeared of flying, would arrive in your gleaming chauffeured state financed automobile. But in front of their constituents they'd be themselves wracked with humility. And never mind your black tie dinners at the Big man's mansion and being greeted at the door by a butler. All in all they'd be fairly decently reasonable and wise men. With a few of your brilliant and even wiser women among them. And both wanting to get the political pulse of the people. They'd also be having to keep their wits about them and be abstemious in imbibing the bottle. And would never be looking as if the shine of their shoes was taken off by having just pee'd all over their boots. They'd too be highly discreet people who would take the trouble to go out in the middle of a meadow to whisper a secret in someone's ear. Nor would you, outside of a parliamentary forum, ever hear them shouting or kicking up an unparliamentary fuss. And it would be no mystery why some of the greatest politicians since Caesar himself, are Irishmen. And included among them, women. Some of whom you might even call Cleopatra.

But powers too that be in the land and wielding influence and omnipresent always and everywhere up and down the main street of every town would be your shop keeper and publican. These manipulators and king makers preside if not behind their counters, then in the back of their shops where they keep tabs on everybody coming and going. And never mind that there are now more than a few supermarkets all over the place. There would still be these smaller emporiums intact, of shoe shops, butchers, drapers, and newsagents, whose proprietors, pillars of decorum and discretion, would with their deposited funds accumulated over the years in the bank and contributors to conspicuous charities, be able to send mightily influential whispers about the village, town or city. But in talking a little bit further about behind the scenes wire pulling there would also be your widespread professional class, the members of which would be the intimate knowers of secrets. Accountants, solicitors, medical and veterinary doctors, and then your dentists, surgeons, and high ranking police, army, or being that this is an island in the sea, maybe even naval officer. All of whom could by a wink or a nod drop the hint to whom it concerned that the time was ripe to put the boot into your man or otherwise blacken his prospects.

So the wise tendency here in this land is to make your enemies carefully and if possible, to do the impossible, and not make an enemy at all. But if you do incur enmity, mark your man well for he'll be somewhere eternally conspiring. So it is always cogent to make sure you yourself never give up putting paid to the son of a bitch where or whenever he dares rear his sneaky ugly head. Plus watch out for his wife if he's got one who'd be busy spreading the spoken if not chemical poison. And never mind the long list of any of the foregoing wielders of influence. For the power any of them exert is still nothing like that found in the family tribe of brothers and sisters, aunts and uncles and which only fades a bite when you come to your second and third cousins and even here you'd best keep a weather eye out for your clannish loyalty. Which, like a pebble in a pond, sends alerting waves across the parish and province to every relative's ear. And never mind what you've heard about the Mafia. For by god as sure as the grass is green in Ireland and the sky only occasionally blue, you would as foreigner or stranger committing a misdeed, be inviting nearly the entire nation to be taking an enemy's side against you with this and that fucker's sworn oath to get you before either of you went to your grave. And as a man you wouldn't want to steal someone's wife unless he wanted to get rid of her. Or as a woman open up your legs for someone's husband. But ah you'd ask, how has the place kept even half way civilised and the whole country not gone one hundred per cent totally haywire before this, and still retains a modicum of the kind of sophistication now demanded by your American tourist. And the answer is easy. And once was very obvious. For the fact was that for many of your years past, above and beyond and dominant in influence over all, were your eternally patient and vigilant clergy. The bishops, parsons, priests, the nuns and religious in general. And not always of the Roman Catholic variety. It is they who from their churches, monasteries and convents have waged a long continual war against obscenity, indecency and fornication. And who have, exhorting from their pulpits, attempted to maintain ethical standards among the population in the face of prevalent fraud, theft and deceit. For in a land long dominated by the invader the habit of lying has become firmly established. And as a traveller on the road asking a direction you'd be forewarned not to believe everything you hear as to getting to your destination. But by god at the same time you'd come across an honesty right for two these days in a nation now going madly modern out of its mind, exposed as it is to the round the clock new social and sexual freedoms broadcast from abroad down out of the skies. Where once only God with his brogue was speaking up there.

Now in the latter case of your concupiscence, here's a type of little story of not that long ago of what you might now expect to confront you in the land of saints and scholars and which erupts as such occasionally does among your mixed semi professional classes pretending to profess a certain amount of broadminded permissiveness. You'd have, coming as you do, and with some frequency, from England and the U.S.A., damsels easy of virtue and wily in the ways of flattering men to the point of forcing them to sit down immediately to hide the embarrassment of their erections. Now this nature of lady would have her skin tight wardrobe and diaphanous garments to fit any occasion, and maybe in extreme cases even her own sports car so as to be seen wearing her haute couture snug arsed clinging short skirt as she got in and out of her racy vehicle. And in so doing be inciting the appetites of every red blooded

Irishman within whose long repressed sight she came. And by god would some of the less religious of them be apoplectically panting and totally indifferent to the bedouin atmosphere of every man's breeches looking like a tent. Nor would she be very much concerned taking notice of the glowering Irish women who would watch her lead the men away. Of course, let it be said, not perhaps for decency's sake, but for the geometric difficulties that might be in it, your newcomer seductress would only be taking on one man at a time. Now we must not confuse this incident about to be told with the more common and accepted occasion when in Ireland saucy shenanigans occur during the likely time of the fox hunt when the blood's up and the hooves are pounding over the turf. It is well known that, with the huntsman's horn sounding, and the hounds giving tongue and the blood lust occasioned by the fox desperately attempting to escape with its life, that this is exactly the time when your interloping foreign lady, her breeches tight over the arse and thighs straining locked over the ribs of her mount leads a likely gent off to the side, well away from the line of the fox. And there dismounted in a sheltered glade, bottoms al fresco do be bouncing. Now this kind of congress is fully understood to happen when members of the opposite sex of the hunt, roused out of their normally private inhibitions, will have at each other in a singularly sexual way with pairs of them flagrantly in copses all over the countryside pounding on top of each other goodo. No, this is not what we are referring to here at all. And in the present situation about to be related, it's all suburban types and cars and not a horse in sight.

Now as we universally know, it's the rich what gets the

pleasure, it's the poor what gets the pain. And in Ireland it's long been the case that outside fox hunting circles, it's the natives get the celibacy and the visitor who more often gets the hanky panky. However, recently in this relatively new nation it has been increasingly your affluent professional business folk who are getting their fair share of licentious shenanigans. And who do in their present lifestyles have champagne delivered to the door of a morning with the milk. And who can, out of the blue, get laid at your company picnics. Especially when a vicar's daughter straight from England shows up and is conversationally everywhere boasting of her multiple orgasms as if she were the only one on the face of the earth so singularly blessed. In any event she wasn't shy in letting it be known that she, given the appropriate Irishman, was ready and willing for a gallop. A nice enough and friendly and generous girl she was. Who'd give you a wondrous smile with the great set of teeth she had gleaming in her head. And arriving in a tight red outfit at the business picnic, didn't she with her plunging neckline soon disappear in what was the early twilight of the afternoon and go off with your genuine homegrown exhilarated Irishman to a nearby glade. Now let me tell you there's little or nothing incognito, confidential or unrevealed in this land and the pair of them would be watched going by more eyes than you could imagine could be in the thirty seven or so heads present. And all but one relishing what was about to unfold.

And so, begob, the scene was set. Accumulating in the nearby bushes and shrubberies was a small crowd waiting in peaceful silence as the pair of intending lovers had already unlawfully presented themselves to each other without clothes and were exposing mammary, urinary and excretary

organs contrary to standards of public decency. And it
wasn't long before the observing little gathering were waiting clucking their mouths at the gymnastic sexual
shenanigans taking place before their very eyes and imported free of custom duty by a member of the British,
leisured, upper middle class. Of course in spite of the
wrenched, twisted and trampled foliage, not everything
going on between the carnal collaborators could be seen
through the leafy undergrowth. But enough to know that
their legs were entwined around each other's necks and
their heads attending to each other's bifurcations. There
was even to be witnessed a little bit of your imported
English bondage. Didn't your seductress ask your man to
tether her wrists and ankles with your man's company tie
and then give her a few lashes across her bottom with her
belt. And who should now at that very moment of the
strap landing, suddenly choose to join this little group of
voyeurs but your man's furiously enraged Irish wife.

Now, amazingly, because of the revered Saint Bridget
goddess of fertility, the Irish believe it can bring a curse
upon you for interrupting sexual intercourse. So there is no
ranting and raving and screaming, 'stop doing that to my
husband'. And in silence the wife furiously fumed there, as
the seductress, stung into action by her chastisement, was
loose once more from her restraint and had got up on her
supine husband to gyrate like a spinning top teetering in
the last of its revolutions. However, it was known at the
picnic that this lady seducer so presently busily nakedly
entwined, came in her own low slung motor vehicle that
she managed to recently purchase brand new with money
she got out of her last divorced husband. And wasn't it on
its four innocent extra wide wheels, parked not that far

away. So didn't some of the ladies of the voyeuristic gang in the bushes steal away while the rest continued watching with patient interest as your lithe seductress assumed a lady dog position and wagging her arse had now your man up on her from behind pumping away like a steam locomotive piston. And busy as both of them were, neither gave any notice to events happening less than fifty yards away. For let me tell you it's one thing in Ireland to quietly and in the customary manner copulate but quite another when you get up to masochistic bondage, gymnastic gyrations and canine machinations. All of which add fuel to the fury of these Irish women of the group now volunteering to avenge the outrage perpetrated upon this temporarily, as it were, deserted wife. Now you'd feel sorry for the poor spouse whose husband is having a jolly dickens of an old time enjoying himself with this self proclaimed multi orgasmic vicar's daughter. Don't worry, come uppance is coming. And there they all are now, already ganged up on the fancy fucking seductress's motor car. And a shiny brilliant red it is too.

If your sensibilities are tender towards your beautiful mechanical equipage, don't watch or listen to what is happening next. Splat. That was a massive cake of gravelly mud flung two handedly on the gleaming bonnet. Crash. That was a large stone just thrown through the windscreen. Smash. That latter reverberation was a big red brown brick you just heard go through the aerodynamically sloped rear window. Boom, boom, boom. Those are boulders heaved pockmarking your deep and sundry dents all over the car roof and body. And the hiss you hear is the air coming out of every last one of the tyres and not sparing the spare one. Plus the gang of lady avengers have just twisted off the outside rear view mirrors specially provided on the front fenders. And through the smashed side windows, they are now able to open up the vehicle's previously locked doors. Having gained access to the perfumed interior, honey from the picnic baskets is now being poured over the cowhide upholstery. And generous fistfuls of butter are being rubbed over any of the honey free spots remaining. All those coloured wires you see pulled out were once connected to the ignition and wrapped colourfully around the gear shift, only god knows what they are connected to now. But one of your men is presently crying out that there's no sugar left for tea. And he's right. Every last bit of it has been poured down into the vicar's daughter's petrol tank, which rumour has it, is guaranteed not to improve the efficiency of the reputed three hundred horse power or thereabouts of this racy vehicle one little bit and they might as well have dropped a two ton boulder or two from a far height on top of the engine. Now as the guilty, recently copulating couple, dressed now, innocently wander back to the picnic site licking their chops, you'd wonder why these clannish Irish women instead of systematically destroying the seductress's motor car, couldn't have been a little more sophisticatedly urbane and simply have made a few of your more pointed remarks reeking of innuendo which would have allowed your seductress to get on her way to other conquests instead of being comforted by your man as she stands there at the side of her Ferrari, head in her hands, sobbing uncontrollably. But I'll tell you why.

Let us go back a little bit to the days of yore. Such Irish women, as do the sons, come from mothers who as they say, slaved their fingers to the bone to give their children always that little better than they had. And let me tell you it's true. And it's become a litany repeated in the kitchens of Irish mothers all over the globe. These resolute, battle hardened females who have formed the character of the Irish woman and her dedication to her home and children which is nearly without parallel in this part of the presently known solar system. And such singleness of purpose is there to this day to prove it. Herself then would recognise this threat to the peace and sanctity of the Irish home from this interloping vicar's daughter gifted with the facility and artistry of fancy fucking. And her slightly more frigid than frivolous sisters in arms would take up to make sure this nimble expert in sexual gymnastics would never dare dream to approach near the aggrieved lady's husband, or that of any other Irishwoman's, again. Nor himself begob step out of line with any more of your liberally lewd foreign ladies. For himself, like all genuine Irishmen, is ever ready to get amorously excited, and as the old saying goes, one Irishman in the bed is like a thunderstorm in a desert that would only come once in a blue moon but by god when he did he would wash away all the sand dunes. And of course it is this nature of the beast that took herself once up the aisle in her lacy veils and had the priest pronounce them man and wife, and he was let loose at her over the honeymoon. Well she soon had enough of that I'm telling you and the law was laid down and the nagging started. And to be fair minded, is it any wonder that himself began escaping out to the pub the nights running without end. And if there was a wage packet its contents would be sadly diminished and swept one way over the mahogany bar as the drink came flowing back in the other direction. So as you might imagine the Mrs. wouldn't soon be getting a gift of a glittering diamond tiara or anything remotely in the way of

jewellery, or a new ring slipped on her finger as she lay
sleeping. But by god what she might get however, and it
wouldn't come gift wrapped, is a fist delivered in the gob,
and any of the sparkling she would see would be
delusionary stars. For as a few more belts and cuffs landed
she'd hear the roar of your man's voice shaking the kitchen
window panes with his proclamation,

"Now will you shut up your gob."

And remember, your man prior to the wedding bells
was as free as a leaf in the breeze and blown hither and
thither constantly. And here he is, hardly over the honeymoon and in the thick of the marriage hearing unforgettable carping and nearly unending pestering quibble.
Nagging, why wasn't he this? Nagging, why didn't he do
that? And, stop making that chewing noise when you chew.
Now of course she'd only be trying to do her best to
improve your man and break him of his worst indoor
vulgar habits. But it is in the nature of the beast that no
Irishman who has ever been put by an Irish mother on this
earth, takes eternal guff from anybody. Or for the matter
of that, one regrets to have to say it, needs to be changed
for the better. For remember he had an Irish father too.
And he'd have from this latter a sense of humour, a sense
of fair play, and a ruddy good damn idea how to laugh,
drink, sing and enjoy himself. And human enough too, for
what awful harm would it be for him to occasionally fall
prey to fancy fucking when it came in a tight red skirt and
Ferrari his way. And so by god when he went home of an
evening, if praise, worship and adoration be not his lot nor
a gentle reassuring caress favoured by Danish women to
give their men under the balls, then the least he wanted
was peace and quiet and if your woman was not content to

give him that by god why wouldn't he raise a ruction and let fly blows in the direction of your woman to shut her nagging speaking hole. That he'd prefer was put to use for something licentious.

And sad to say all this has led to a strange kind of phenomenon in Ireland. Friday being the nights on which it all occurs, filled as it is with this distressing form of mayhem. With the lady of the house home waiting of this Friday payday evening for himself to return the worse for drink. And she knows by god he's going to make an attempt to jump on her. And that from such might come further childer in profusion. And she would be thinking it would be nearly better to get a fist instead. And that it would be up to her to get enough food, have shelter and provide clothing by scraping, saving and scrimping and sacrificing to keep the childer as neat and clean and well fed as any household or childer could be kept. And she would. But by god there would still come that ould Friday night. As back from the pub reels himself growling and roaring after an evening's jolly male camaraderie with the usual slaps on the back and the encouragement into the future as the great dream boats are launched sailing on those wondrous seas of alcohol. And there are words long coined into a phrase to describe what happens next.

"To bate sick the poor wife stupid."

And as himself approaches up the front path, fear spreads throughout the household. In the poor woman's panic bolts are thrown as the front ingress is securely locked. But nothing is safe from this returned cursing reveller who is already kicking and finally with a bull rush of the shoulder smashes the door open, sending it swinging askew on its now twisted hinges. Children huddle in the bedrooms as a cry goes through the house,

"Come here till I get holt of you, you bitch."

And many a lady it is who would have already escaped out the back kitchen door or had she been trapped up in a bedroom, down the drainpipe and into the back garden. Here to be crouched in fear and trembling. And woe if she had no back garden or attic to be retreating to. And found herself instead cowering and shivering in terror of her life in a closet or under the bed, her lot at that exact moment at least made easier due to the special strength Irishwomen derive from prayer. And although it is no picnic past midnight or in the wee hours outdoors in the wintry wind and rain she'd have the company of other similar stranded ladies in their pyjamas and kimonos waving sheepishly back. And what the hell, all of them had at least escaped a thumping and could steal back inside to a sofa when himself was comatose asleep.

But these recent days come to pass there is no need to feel fatally sorry for such women and their lot. For as a result of such long borne heinousness there is a new Irishwoman afoot in this land. Of two varieties. And both by god are wearing the trousers with a vengeance. And they are of the very latest phenomenon in female evolution. And just to put a quick handy name on them you'd have to call them Man Fighters. They are respectively Man Fighter Mark I and Man Fighter Mark II. Such as these let me tell you would make your most ardent military feminists all over the rest of the globe seem like a bunch of polite male worshipping angels. And by god, let me tell you if you meet one, be assured there are plenty more where she came from. But let us first take your variety, of your Man Fighter Mark I. She'd be of a prankish type and ready for a guffaw as your man knocking down the front door fell straight into his spaghetti dinner waiting for him just inside on the floor with his face rearing up out of the red sauce your woman would be up on top of the staircase, slapping her knees as she roared hysterically laughing her head off.

Now then your man might kick and dance around a bit and be back as usual next night in the pub. But your woman Mark I would still have yet another little subtle trick up her apron as your man again delayed indefinitely out in the pub. This time she'd get the dinner nice and ready and hot out of the oven. The spaghetti heaped up so. The baked potato, two of them steaming cracked open at the side of the plate. The red sauce cascaded generously over the top of the lot. And then she'd nice as you please, saunter straight down to the pub, where your man is holding forth with his enthralled admiring cronies and suddenly there in front of him is placed his dinner, with a tiny little heap of your baby mushrooms right under his very nose and your Mark I Man Fighter woman without so much as a word has just disappeared out the door. Now you'd find that not too many of your men would like a repeat of this in a hurry.

But your Man Fighter Mark II is a rather different kettle of fish altogether. And is usually in a single, divorced or separated condition and entrepreneurially emerging in the rag trade, motor, publishing, journalism, stockbroking or bloodstock industries. Who could, if they continue to proliferate, turn Ireland into a male masochist's paradise. Two fisted, these ladies with sleeves rolled up have been known in the sex act to swiftly without warning imprison their lovers in scissor wrestling grips, squeezing their male opponents till they scream for mercy, or agree to become male doormats upon which they can wipe their feet indefinitely. Ah but your Mark II Man Fighter is encountering stubborn resistance from your Irishman who has no intention of being ordered around for the rest of his life, and he does more than occasionally fight back instead of letting out a plaintive sob for merciful discontinuance. But these are the new women of a recently new nation who would ensure that if himself dared to present his dirty socks he would promptly get them back across the face. And many of your men without clean hosiery to wear went barefoot in their shoes so as not to smell up the office where they work. And even as the television was switched on of a supposedly peaceful evening, it was what she wanted to watch, and by gob when she was finished it was both of them to bed. Where likely as not your man innocently sleeping would dream the offending socks were now draped across his nose. And he'd get an elbow in the ribs for snoring. These are the women who at their dinner parties arrange for the ladies to be served and for the men to have to get up and help themselves and who make the temporary men they encounter make their tea and coffee of a morning and demand they deliver it up to them with their own private newspaper to read as they lie in bed easy as you please. And suddenly horny your Mark II Man Fighter is then demanding of your man to get a bugle on him that would whip a donkey out of a sandpit. Now it doesn't take much psychology to appreciate that your poor chap standing there is shame faced and flaccid in his flute and wouldn't be able to raise enough stiffness to lift a feather. Even if he had a railroad derrick helping and a bit of dynamite blowing his prick towards the sky.

Now for the sake of peace and a beautiful place to live

with plenty to eat and drink, your occasional man will go along with taking this kind of awful guff. But soon finds himself finally exasperated by this routine and previously used to his ould mother's ways and fed up now to the teeth, he at last in the true Irish tradition raises a fist to give this Man Fighting woman an old fashioned and deserving one in the gob. A big and fatal mistake. For sure hasn't herself this long time past taken up and become proficient in your martial arts of judo, jujitsu and karate. And here she is standing already nakedly up out of the bed, well balanced on her strong thighed legs and already winding up to launch her own sizzling left hook of a karate chop to contuse your poor old hombre one hell of an explosive blow on his own surprised gob. Plus, often as not, following it up with her knee cap plunging into his ruddy unprotected goolies which collapses your man and leaves him to lie writhing on the sheepskin rug covering the floor. The rest of his nightmare life now to be filled with visions of these Amazonian ladies who so long denied their rights have now understandably become the hostile eyed, karate chop emasculators you see now loose in the cities of Ireland building their big businesses, making male subordinates cower as they issue their biddings, and enticing other unsuspecting males to jump up on them and get their pricks caught in a mangle, the squeezing of which would make a shark's jaws feel like a caress in paradise. Now you might say the status quo of Ireland is wrecked forever beyond all recognition as these brave new breed of ladies lay waste around them, making their presence known with multicoloured publicity and at dawn kicking the men who have survived the night out of their warm beds to find hotels or to go home to their wives while their own private maids bring them their own private breakfasts. And by god on top of it all, some of these two fisted Mark II Man Fighters also have men lawyers at the ready speeding the shafts of writs deep into the heart of the male chauvinist enemy and suing and threatening to sue the living bigoted bejesus out of them. And you'd sometimes be glad there's only a random Mark II Man Fighter you'd see encroaching out into the more rural landscape and sitting up on tractors and digging drainage ditches.

Ah but don't give up on your Irishman yet. And don't worry about the countryside. There are still to be found in enough plenitude those stalwarts who do not cower, who do not wince, who do not hold their hands shielding their goolies. And who as men still stand upright and resolute at the bar over which their time honoured pint or ball of malt is pushed under their chins while talking the evening away without so much a backward thought given to the Man Fighter Mark I or your bloody well more difficult Mark II variety, or what either of these categories have wrought. And let me tell you there's no whining or whinging about washing an anciently dirty pair of socks or the underpants with the slight green mould alive on them. Or not having your bowl of steaming spuds on the table with buckets of butter and pucks of cabbage when it's time to eat. But of course she might, while you are up on top of her doing what comes naturally, be reading over your shoulder the in memoriams in the evening newspaper. But even in the face of such indifference there are still left plenty of your Irishmen who carry on doing what the bull does to the cows and even if the latter is not reading a newspaper sure she's often busying herself eating grass.

And in Ireland
Nourishment and concupiscence
Often
Go together
And more praise be
To the
Small farm
Where
It happens

THERE IS IN IRELAND NO GREATER POWER THAN
THE POWER OF THE WOMAN, WHO FROM THE
LONG YEARS SHE RESOLUTELY ANCHORS HERSELF
IN HER HOME, IS ALWAYS READY WITH THE
CUPS OF TEA AND A HOSPITALITY THAT
ENCOURAGES LIFE.

VI

Ah but let us for the delayed moment not yet allude to
leaping leprechauns wearing their golden little boots and
emerald jackets and tall orange hats and dancing their little
dances on grassy mounds in the moonlight but instead
focus on the saints. Now there is nowhere on earth where
more praying goes on for favours to be granted from the
above than on the isle of the shamrock. And using the
intercession of these sainted holy folk, there'd be your long
columns in the papers of Deo Gratias, and thanks be to
Sancta Trinitas, St. Jude, St. Anthony, St. Christopher and a
list of the hallowed consecrated persons as long as your
arm. And according to the publication promised, doing
your miracles left right and centre. Now I know among
you you'd have your sceptics. But by god there's one saint
I'm telling you who for a fact didn't leave someone's prayer
and fervent request unanswered. And it's astonishing that
hardly do you ever see her name mentioned in the columns

of thanksgiving. And I'm not talking about St. Clare of St. Martha but St. Bridget herself. Who long before she ever had anything to do with your sanctification and the Catholic religion, was more than rumoured to be the ancient pagan goddess of fertility.

Now you would, if not of the Roman Catholic persuasion, be forgiven if you were a might bit sceptical about the powers of these saints whose names are invoked up and down long lists in the newspapers. But let me tell you, you are making one hell of a big mistake. And plenty of the disasters and yearning in your life could be put right. For when he was still Blessed Oliver Plunkett, and not yet canonized as a saint, there was no end of requests this eminently Blessed man was getting from all sides and for which he interceded. And weren't acknowledgements of thanks to him published one following the other in the columns of the better Irish papers, for an avalanche of favours received. And this Blessed man whose preserved head in a tabernacle I visited in Drogheda, did much in saving the idolatrous bacon of yours truly with miracles of a nature I won't go into now. And didn't the same Blessed Oliver, as he was then, do the same for all those to whom I recommended him. And in due course, following successful deliverance from ruinous misfortune, didn't he later become the patron saint of Sebastian Balfe Dangerfield, the notorious Ginger Man himself.

Now then. You Protestants, you Buddhists, you Jews, you Muslims, you Hindus, you Shakers, get ready. Here's a true story referring to an absolute miracle. The like of which and considering the circumstances, is not often described in Ireland due to the religious devoutness of the people and due to the many celibate spiritual exercises in which the populace more normally indulges. And although this little tale might be considered by some to be somewhat bizarrely pagan in nature, if not a wee bit satanic or heretic, it is nevertheless religious enough in its sincerity. Nor is there the merest bit of exaggeration here about what happened and it is recounted just to show the power of the Saints, and especially your St. Bridget who comes out with flying colours.

Now there was this old, not to say ancient friend who some would, and many did, refer to as Mr Ireland himself. A well built man of charm and intelligence from a prominent professional and farming family well reputed in their rural parish. And whom I had not met for this many a long year gone past. But whom I had remembered was reputed all over Dublin city as one of the great swordsmen of his time. And it was no surprise to anybody that with his ready smile and generally jovial nature, he was a great excitement for the women and they especially for him. And it would be no exaggeration to say that your Mark I, and II, women, were they around at the time would have beat a path to his door ready to wait on him hand and foot, washing, drying and mending his socks be they got as green from wearing as a shamrock. And wasn't it equally a fact that your man throughout his vigorous youth was obsessed ecstatic by any likely looking lass. Not unnatural enough you might say. Well now much of your grunting and groaning of ecstasy has with the years gone past floated away like music out on the ether. And your man Mister Ireland himself was left a father of more children than he cared to count, and they were fully grown up now, and members in good standing of the Irish nation. And he himself was getting on a bit. Just that little extra long in the tooth, slightly greyer in the

head, stiffer in the limbs. But by god still stiff where he'd
more than occasionally continued to want to be. And his
lust for the women wasn't fading in the least. Now when
semi retirement time came from the stimulating occupation
of breeding race horses, didn't he with his huge nest egg
buy himself a little cottage in the far west where contentedly betimes he would go and where betimes there'd be a
hooley or two and your singing and dancing in the town's
local pubs. And were betimes too with Ireland's growing
world wide reputation for grand music there'd be coming
along from foreign places a likely lass or two whom by a
small kindness he might courteously inveigle to come back
to the hospitality of his cottage to there be entertained in
the cosy safe surroundings infused with your wellbeing and
togetherness that comes from having a deep serious discussion about the Irish weather.

Now then. Where's the miracle in all that, you're asking. But I'd ignore the question and detour here to have
take note all men edged a little bit past their prime. For
your grey headed Mister Ireland out in the pub most
evenings would have to wait for the young lasses to choose
their willing partners before they even deign give him a
tumble. But such was your man's charm together with his
patient persistence with more of your courteous kindness
and assistance, that enough of the young ladies sought his
jovial accommodating company. And there soon were one
or two of the young ladies who became firm platonic
friends. A fat lot of good that did him, you're saying.
However, wasn't there one particular young attractive Ger-
manic lady who more than anything else wanted to get
married and have children. And she said to your totally and
absolutely atheistic Mister Ireland that someone had told

her of a St. Bridget to whom such a request of a husband and family might be made and her recent year or two of anguish be ended. Now your Mister Ireland threw his head back with a burst of laughter, sure what Saint had he ever beseeched could even tell him the month it was in the year never mind finding a husband for her. Nevertheless as she was about to return to Germany, he'd be more than happy to escort her up over the hill beyond to where there was known to be a St. Bridget's Well. And where, why not, you can write out your request on a scrap of paper and throw it into the waters and at least dream of your request being granted. And your man Mister Ireland a pagan disbeliever from the age of his puberty thought what the hell, here is a Saint who was once a Celtic pagan goddess, while your young German girl was sending in her entreaty why not himself write out on a bit of paper his own petition and flick it into the water along with hers? At least to himself, and being that he was asking could he be delivered soon of a piece of arse, it would be a good old laugh and a miracle to boot.

Now a month went by and then two and finally a stormy autumn afternoon a letter came from Frankfurt, Germany from your young lady which your Mister Ireland read with wide eyed amazement if not disbelief. Lo and behold didn't your Fraulein get picked up hitch hiking the day after the visit to the well and three weeks later got married to a prosperous engineer and wasn't she now sitting comfortable in a bijou residence in the best part of town and pregnant as she wrote. And didn't she say further words full of appreciation for St. Bridget and that she sincerely hoped he had also got what he had requested in his petition that he had tossed into the well. And didn't Mister

Ireland sit reading with delight this letter in his cottage and
as it was growing dark and the night brought with it
greater gales lashing up against the coast and shaking the
land, himself thought it the ideal time to sit down in front
of the glowing turf fire and answer your German girl's letter. Sure on this very day wasn't it his birthday com-
memorating more years on this earth than he presently
cared to count. In the cold wind and lashing rain he'd taken
his usual six mile hike up over the nearby mountain and
had a raging appetite. And being a great wine connoisseur
wasn't he cooking himself a bit of a gourmet dinner and he
had cooling for himself outside on the doorstep a bottle of
champagne to accompany the plate full of smoked salmon
he had sliced and surrounded with choice bits of shelled
lobster caught that day not more than two hundred yards
away down in the depths off the coast. A great thick slab
of your best sirloin steak also awaited to be grilled over the
fire. To be washed down with a grand booming burgundy
decanted on the sideboard. To his previous platonic German lady he had in brackets already appended to his letter:
    "Wish you were here to join me in my little lonely
party. But meanwhile more power and praise be to St.
Bridget, and it is well for you, and I still fervently hope the
highly unlikely wish I want granted happens to me one of
these days."
    And for the sentiment that was in it, he had on his
record player the great Irish tenor Frank Patterson singing
'Abide With Me' and 'Ave Maria'. And he was really enjoying composing his communication in this musical
atmosphere of piety. But let me tell you, before he fully
answered and got to the last word of his letter expressing
his delight with her developments and the bestowment

upon her of the favour asked of St. Bridget, suddenly there was a ferocious thunderclap, the whole cottage shaking and the lights went out and Frank Patterson's singing stopped and the sitting room was plunged into darkness, as were the few lights that were usually visible in the town two miles away. He lit several candles around the room and continued to write his letter on the board over his knee, describing the wax blob which had just fallen on the paper as being from an ecclesiastic candle he'd bought specially to burn during dinner if he ever had the good luck to find another girl as pleasant as she had often been to cook for and have dinner with. Then he was interrupted in his reminiscing by what he thought were gusts of wind shaking the door. But then as he continued to listen, he realized the thumping was a knock. And he got up from the fireside from where he was writing his letter and went over to the door to open it, thinking aloud that bejesus god almighty who'd be out on the highway and calling on me on a night the like of this.

Now remember, in the West and during a storm, Ireland is one hell of a wild and lonely place, and you wouldn't be outside having casual visitors on a night as the one raging outside where the salt from the sea spray breaking on the cliffs beyond was tasting on your lips. But forever generous and willing with his hospitality like anyone in the West would be, without caution he undid the latches and slowly opened the door as the gale and rain swept in. And by the faint light he could see nothing. Then came an almighty flash of lightning directly above in the sky which hit the steeple of an isolated small Protestant chapel down the road. And there revealed in the deluge coming down, as your man was straining peering out from the door of the cottage, was a figure in a yellow sou'wester, with a shepherd's crook and a backpack on the back and stout walking boots on the feet and a foreign sounding soft melodic female voice.

"Forgive me sir for troubling you. I am lost. And I look for The Seaside Hotel I cannot find. I am apologising for disturbing you but perhaps you could direct me. I would be so grateful. I am Swedish."

"Come in, come in out of the rain, for god's sake and don't be standing out there in the gales, thunder and lightning. Swedish or not."

"Thank you. But I do not wish to disturb you."

"Disturb me. Nonsense. Come in. And welcome."

Your grateful Swede, raindrops cascading down her exquisite face, smiled a relieved smile of thanks and hesitated no further over this unexpected invitation to enter into the dry warm fireglow and candlelight of the cottage. Now we won't go too deeply into your man's age of that of the young Swedish girl. Suffice to say she was a slender blonde of medium height with soft lustrous grey blue eyes, and he was certainly old enough not only to be her father but even old enough to give her the benefit of grandfatherly protection should she need it. But also suffice to say that as your Swede stood there surveying a grinning Mr. Ireland there was another lightning flash overhead and thunderclap that made it sound as if the roof of the cottage had just exploded off. And your man Mr. Ireland opened his arms as the girl jumped forward in fear as the rumble of the thunder echoed back from the surrounding hillsides.

Well now your man Mr. Ireland, although he could believe his ears, he couldn't really believe his eyes, and was ruddy well delighted out of his mind at the golden haired apparition he now released from his protective arms. And he was grateful to have some company, however brief, on a stormy night, which even as he stood there thinking of the present wonderment, was increasing in ferocity. And while excusing himself to take a pee, he did in fact in the water closet, give himself a belt on the forehead with the heel of his hand to make sure this was still his own brain thinking in his old grey head on this the top end of this body. But sure enough, as luck was now rapidly having it and returned from the water closet, there she was removing from her shoulders the dripping wet backpack. And off came her hat. And then her sou'wester. Then her thick Aran Island sweater revealing two braided long golden locks of hair now hanging down her back nearly to her hips. Her hands and knuckles were red-blue with cold.

Now there was no trace of Man Fighter Mark I, II or for the matter of that Mark III or IV in your young girl, as your man Mister Ireland led her across the room to the glowing turf fire. And as she smilingly stood there with the sudden whooshes of wind gusting up the chimney your man quick as a flash had in off the doorstep the bottle of champagne and with a ceremonial pop, filled and was handing your Swedish beauty a glass. Which she took gratefully enough and by god downed in one delighted gulp. And then in the warmth she removed another sweater. Which left your man's mouth suddenly salivating with shock. For in the cerulean blue cotton shirt she wore he could see the distinct outline upon her chest of exactly the ideal of all the breasts, the image of which he had ever had the temerity to conjure up in his dreams. And not that his own good Irish mother had ever deprived him. However, and notwithstanding, didn't your man Mister Ireland find he suddenly had a horn on him that would not only whip your Irish donkeys out of sandpits but would lever an African elephant up out of an Irish bog. And by god, so as not to inhospitably intimidate or alarm your poor Swedish stray just in out of the storm, your man had to sit down in a hurry. For over these past nearly three years of recent celibacy and to those ladies he was dying to fuck, he never once showed any of them anything but courtesy, kindness and consideration. And thanking him for his flattery these same young women with equal courtesy, kindness and consideration declined his invitations to bed.

Now then. The hotel your sweet young beauty was looking for was but a mere two miles away on the sea road, half of which by now was sure to be washed away by the ocean waves. But your man had his boots, a torch and his own sou'wester and didn't he know a shortcut of only a quarter of a mile to the hostelry by footpath over the nearby hill. And so as your young lady had now caught her breath the temptation to tell a lie was desperate. But he did not yield. For it had long been his forthright honesty that the ladies had always come to love about him best. So despite the rain, lightning and lashing gale he was without subterfuge about to offer to accompany her over the hill to her hotel. However at least he felt he deserved the pleasure of a little delay, and anyway your splendid Swede was already saying in her wonderful Elizabethan voice,

"I am, sir, from Uppsala. Where I study about moss and lichen at the university."

Well the grin on your Mister Ireland's countenance stopped your Swede in her tracks, for it went from behind one ear to behind the other. And she wondered what she could have said to produce such radiant joy on this gentleman's face. And you won't believe this. But Mister Ireland had, tucked away right there in his library located in the corner of this room, some of the greatest scholarly tomes ever written about mosses and lichen. And not only that. There wasn't much to be known that he didn't know already about your Bryophyta and the similar but unrelated lichen. And without saying a word he beckoned her over to his library shelves where were, as he pointed out, the six leather-bound volumes of the most brilliant authoritative texts ever written about mosses and lichens. And she too smiled from behind one ear to behind the other and then broke into an astonished delighted laughter. And let me tell you at that moment the minutes now didn't have any trouble flying by, nor was there any guilt in your man not setting out to hike through the storm to The Seaside Hotel. And as the two of them warmly stood there smiling into each other's eyes your young lady disclosed that she'd specialised in the study of the horn tooth moss. And now your man who knew everything about your species Ceratoden Purureus, gave up worrying about how brief this encounter might be and even dared think of the possible endless hours of discussion to come. And for the first delicate time the name St. Bridget flashed like a lightning bolt across his mind. But just as it did, he dismissed it realizing that this was no time to be deluding himself thinking about the fertility miracles wrought by the Celtic deity.

But in your man now getting slightly apoplectic he did not forget to be the best of hosts and straight away suggested that Katrina, as she was called, go immediately and help herself to a nice hot bath and warm herself up. While he whipped around a bit to put together a spot of supper they could have.

"O no. I could not. You have been far too kind already. I should now try to go find again my hotel."

"Sure after you've eaten the storm may have let up and I'll lead you by the shortcut over the hill."

"I have already taken four glasses of your champagne."

"Actually you've had five and are welcome to more."

"Ooo la la. I did not know I had five. But you should not now have to cook for two. I must not please put you to so much trouble."

"This is Ireland where you wouldn't be worrying about a foolish thing like that. I'd be offended for you not to join me. And sure, since when was meeting a fellow botanist trouble? Besides it is my birthday."

"O how underbar, that is how we say wonderful in Swedish."

"Well underbar, that's settled now. And now I am not too keen that you should be let go again out in this storm. And in that door there is another bedroom. And yours for the night. And let me assure you there is no need for there to be any compromising or any embarrassing proximity to be caused to anyone invited to stay."

"I stay for your birthday. Thank you so much. Now I go bath."

And despite her protestations over invading his privacy and taking up his time it was a whole hour later when she again presented herself bathed and fragrant in a sweater and skirt and ready to have another glass of champagne from the second storm chilled bottle brought in from the front door step. For Katrina taught your man how to skol. And never did your man Mister Ireland pick up new Swedish words faster or ever see anyone so hungry or enjoy her food more. And gone in a thrice, washed away with the champagne, was every last bit of the smoked salmon and lobster. And the steak an inch and a half thick. Which she said she would have very rare and which she chewed down with gusto, admitting that she had only eaten an apple and an orange since the evening before.

"I am having such a lovely underbar time."

But now with the steamy baked spuds and a good heap of buttery steamed spinach and gulps of her burgundy wasn't she now able to smilingly tell him between mouthfuls of her life up to date. The boyfriend who only eight months ago blew himself up with a stick of dynamite because she wouldn't marry him. And another whom she also wouldn't marry, now in a mental institution.

"I am a simple girl. I do not know what I do to men which I do not mean to do. It is why I come away and alone to Ireland."

"Ah now, with no shortage of simple men, you've come to the right place."

"Yes I think so. I like to travel. Maybe I miss the skiing. Maybe too I miss the bastu and how one dives then in the cold sea. To collect moss specimens next year I go to visit the rain forests of Brazil."

"Now ·that's a great idea."

As they spoke and drank and spoke some more the storm still raged; the rain peppering the window panes and the wind slamming gusts at the cottage walls and tugging at, and a couple of times nearly lifting off, the thatch of the roof. But during this idyllic impromptu dinner party, they had become like old friends. And up and down he danced delighted attendance upon her, putting a hot water bottle shoved down between the sheets and placing a tome on the tropical lichens by her bedside. And now for the moment, and sure for the night that was in it, why not take the comfort nearest at hand and make herself entirely at home. Have a sup of brandy. And then a good sleep and after breakfast in the morning of pucks of rashers, sausages, eggs and tea, he would in the brand new day walk her to the hotel. Or for the matter of that, anywhere else she cared to go in this local kingdom come. And on the way show her some rare mosses and lichens to boot.

Enough said of any attempted enticement by your man, half sloshed. Katrina was only too delighted to accept the hospitality of a bed for the night. And after singing happy birthday in Swedish to him for the third time, and bowing and smiling to him, she moved her backpack into the spare bedroom. And here he was, your man Mister Ireland, well wined and dined retiring purring with near contentment to his bed. Recalling how, as she got up to retire to her chamber, she came over on tip toe to peck him on each cheek and then one on the forehead. Now you would imagine with the storm still raging and such delectable company less than a few yards away, your Mister Ireland couldn't get himself to sleep in a hurry. And he lay listening to the lashing gale and the explosive thundering of the sea as it trapped air up the long caves extending inland from the bottom of the sea cliffs. Until he fell fast asleep. Deep in a dream of a heavenly angel winged lady in white diaphanous lacy veils hovering in the air over his bed. And didn't he suddenly wake up. And by god wasn't there coming a knocking at his bedroom door. And didn't the door open. And wasn't she herself Katrina standing there in a lacy nightgown.

"Please forgive me for disturbing you. I am sorry but I was frightened to sleep alone. Would you mind if I go in the bed with you?"

Now your man Mister Ireland, hospitable to the last and ready to do any kindness, swept open the covering of the bed, and Katrina like a dream descended in beside him between the sheets. As wasn't he, long before he went to sleep, hoping beyond hope that at the midnight high tide Katrina would be terrified by the ground shaking under the cottage with explosions of the seas in the caves that went in under the shore, and in thinking that the end of the world had come or at the very least an earthquake, would rush into his room in panic. Now every Irishman considering the highly religious nature of the country, has always been eternally grateful for any little taste of a piece of arse he can get. And might do a lot irreligious to get it. But your man Mister Ireland still had his principles of making no overtures to a woman without enthused reciprocation. And he lay still as total death itself beside her. But now, not that many minutes later, didn't Katrina's hand reach for that of Mister Ireland's. And take his fingers slowly and surely up, up, up, to place them upon her warm, silkily soft breast. By god never mind the gales. Or the under the shore detonations. For soon the seas out in the ocean this night were nothing like the bedclothes that started to go up and down. With Mister Ireland having one of the most glorious nights of his entire life. And if he was less than a saint, he was at least betimes in the area of botany, a bit of a scholar. And appropriately enough it is by these two vocations that this isle became known as the Land of Saints and Scholars. And as he in the dawn's early light saw Katrina's startlingly stunning arse wagging its curvaceously white sparkling way to bring him his breakfast in bed, he was no longer the disbelieving pagan infidel of the day

106

A SINGULAR COUNTRY

before. Thanks be to God The Big Himself Of The Brogue
Above and to St. Bridget for favours received.

But now
Don't all of you
At once go
Start praying to this
Celtic deity
And littering her well
With wishes and requests.

PORTENDING THIS VAST AREA OF LONELINESS
WHICH KEEPS THE WEST AWAKE, AMERICA IS
NEVER LOST UPON THE CONSCIOUSNESS AS THE
NEXT PARISH BEYOND THIS BAY AND ACROSS
THIS OCEAN.

VII

Now so that you wouldn't be wondering what's old and what's new and what's next in Ireland, it would be appropriate to confuse the issue further by pronouncing the single overriding fact of the matter of this country is that time is of a strange continuous kind. That envelopes you as you stand at the bar of any half way decent pub, and where you're not unlucky to be left dreaming. And in so far as your yesterday is concerned it was more or less much like it is today and you can be certain by the end of today that it will be no different tomorrow and therefore you'd soon be left thinking for a considerable prolonged period that your life had stopped in its tracks with nothing you ever did or were in the past mattering or worth a damn. And the future will bring about no change. Except ordering up the next round of drinks to toast the memory of someone you kindly recall. Who did what you're doing, only faster.

But of course if you believe any of the above it only

means you didn't read the previous chapter. And if you have read it, I know exactly what you're thinking. It's that Ireland could do with more of your Katrinas wandering in out of storms. And you'd be right. For let me tell you, plenty of your farming Irishmen in the nation are lurking lonely within their cottages waiting and looking for a non Man Fighting variety of wife. And this is what's new. Here and there they've been appearing with this infiltration slowly happening over the last few years, and the foreign influx changing Ireland out of all recognition. With ladies almost resembling the like of Katrina found wandering all over the place from the remote byways to up and down the main street of many a town. Arriving as they do with their backpacks and shepherd's crooks and representing every sort of ethnic variety from your French to your Dutch and from your Finnish to your Icelandic. Here to marvel at, to be exasperated with and to enjoy the uncommon exhilarating nature of this land.

So you can forget now for a second your previous old hat descriptions you've been getting of this country. Even back as far as them ancient scholarly monks scratching their heads isolated praying in their stone huts and diving into freezing cold lakes at dawn of a morning. And disregard the time when the locals were having their dickens of a good time and fun at the expense of himself come over from somewhere else with his grand airs and who waltzed around the ballroom up in the big house, the structure of which, aided and abetted by themselves the natives, was falling into chronic disrepair. But better you might say than your locals applying a torch and conflagrating the whole lot, and putting paid to the fine manners, fine wines and fine paintings within, and turning the place into an inferno glowing in a beautiful warm sight by night on the landscape. And briefly rejoice now that, except for here and there, all that kind or ruinous caper is gone. It is instead the natives getting hot on fire puffing themselves like old steam engines to death on cigarettes and busy inviting the foreigner to come fill these pure skies with lethal fumes. And this is what's next in Ireland. Remembering of course that destruction and self destruction have always been an inclination of the people, on the principle that it is better to be immediately eating and living alive today than it is to be worrying today that you'll be dead and buried on a tomorrow a bit later.

Ah but let us stop any further complaint right here. You wouldn't think it could happen but a new era has dawned. Your marauding speculator who evolves from a class long known as your gombeen man and who with his cache of cash, has long survived upon this isle by being the little shopkeeper, selling your groceries, sweets and minerals, cheese and biscuits and who held all about him in his debt and who in other guises bought and sold and disfigured land and landscape, is in full retreat. For by god hasn't he suddenly found that there's a bit of money to be made out of culture and beauty. And also hasn't there been a louder and louder outcry which came about on another principle: that a farmer himself doesn't mind very, very slowly dying but by god don't in the meantime kill his cattle with lethal fumes before they are ready to go to market. And so now battle lines have been drawn. From one end of the country to the other. Bastions of defence stand, Georgian mansions still to be seen elevated on the horizon with smoke coming out of their chimneys instead of their windows from fires started by the natives. And so here you are in Ireland as

evening approaches. You are looking for accommodation of
the sort to which Katrina was heading before she knocked
on the door of Mister Ireland. And got accommodation
free of charge in his bed. Well you might be asked to pay
something but at least you'll be introduced to the
astonishingly pleasant phenomenon of the Country House
Hotel. Which now affirms victory for the preservation of
elegance and stands as a signal symbol of the revolution for
the better which has hit this land. Great houses, instead of
being in ruins with their ghosts hovering over the dust,
where one can scrape one's shoes on the mud scraper and
enter from the winter's damp cold or a summer's wet chill
to discover inside grandeur and enchantment. And find the
glowing warmth of a turf fire and a woman sitting in her
evening crinolines knitting and crocheting, ancestral eyes
peering down from their portraits approvingly. The drawing room will still have its silk-clothed walls, crystal chandeliers, mirrors, and it gilts gleaming. Sit there over your
champagne and rejoice that instead of finding this mansion
with debris strewn floors over which cattle roam and rub
their necks and shoulders on the great doric columns still
holding up pediments, you can instead cross your legs
reflectively and imagine, were these scratching beasts there,
and you weren't, that in revenge this great edifice would
drop an occasional carved stone cornice down upon the
bullock heads in a nice piece of random justice.

Now then. These present Country House Hotels and
former private mansions and castles are to be marvelled at
where they still occupy the landscape. Standing there only a
little tarnished from their former glory, with not a single
sign of the inmates having to flee out to the front lawn in
their silk pyjamas as fire gutted their homes. Instead any

blazing combustion is confined to the kitchens where there is merrily baking the hotel's own bread. And only an apple's throw away out within the great high walls of the gardens a plethora of vegetables grow leaping fresh and green from the ground. And in the bedrooms, delightful colours delight the eye. Flowers on your bedside table. Steamingly hot water pouring out of taps for your bath, as you recline in the billowing perfumed latherings of soap. And as you dry your back with a big towel you look out the window at the solemnity of these graceful parklands stretching away in the distance. Let me tell you it doesn't half make you purr with the pleasure of still being alive. And a little later as you knock off another bottle of champagne while ordering your meal, you sigh in a final contentment. The Maitre d' is down this very moment in the cellars selecting bottles of wine to be fetched up to your restaurant table to match up with what you've chosen from the menu. And by god some of these vintages which your man has these years stored away will give you plenty of your euphoric paroxysms as you thrill to their bouquet, character, taste and aftertaste and as they set afloat wondrous other anticipations. And mind you, do hold back your mild hysteria over the bill and remember that such exquisite wine doesn't come cheap. But next morning awake after a night of soft pillows and comfortable dry mattresses for sleep, you'll be full enough of satisfaction to stare life right back in the face. And challenge any new nonsense afoot.

And amazingly the very existence of these Country House Hotels has come to reverse the falling down nature of the nation. Somehow the good news of their existence has spread to your ordinary, normally quiet man in the street. Who has finally come to realize that he's got rights in his own country. And can get up on his hind legs to shout that he is himself a living part of a new Ireland dawned. Where the trees, the beauty of architecture, the cleanliness of the air and water and the freedom to open up and read your previously held to be blasphemously dirty book is his to enjoy, never mind the naked view of human bodies. But of course long repressed as he's been, the Irishman has gone overboard as seems to regrettably be the recent case with the insane mad rush to view the most prurient of the most pornographic freshly imported videos that any poor Irish television set has ever scalded its screen with. And sure the shops selling such filthy stuff have erupted everywhere. But in spite of this, and I don't care what or how strong the rumour is, your Irish young lads and lasses are not yet being filmed wearing nothing but shamrock wreaths and writhing lewdly to the rhythm of a ceili band in an Irish effort to manufacture such a product. Not since last Wednesday anyway.

But still there does now pose one of the great human mysteries concerning the devout spiritual nature and the pure mind of the Irish people that such illegal permissiveness should be greeted with such open arms, ears and eyes. Meaning that this island race were, beneath all the moral posturing, always of a liberal nature. And this present letting people see and read a little of what they fancy, has lead to another recent astonishment in the matter. The formerly banned writers who were railed against by the various legions of decency and moral seemliness, have been resurrected along with their books up out of their graves. And the previous image of their once filthy mindedness wiped clean and now polished into gleaming acceptance.

A SINGULAR COUNTRY

And them scribblers as were ridiculed and accused of impurity in the use of the printed word and had as a result their work spitefully destroyed, are now emblazoned in name all over the kip from one end of the country to the other. And begob haven't all their dirty words been forgiven. They are now the lure for the tourist to patronise a restaurant or nightclub and even if not one page of their books is ever opened, turned or read, they can as they eat and drink see up there on the walls an authentic picture of the author himself. Perhaps on his horse or wearing his top hat or even as he was in his grubbier unknown days maybe digging up spuds and often without a smile on his face. And no doubt he wears this latter grim expression because rarely is a penny remitted to his estate - or, if by some miracle he's still alive having survived the rejection and ridicule, paid to himself. Nor are there any royalties forked over on the drinks sold in a pub named after him. Where folk flock to imbibe and reminisce in his memory. You can even begob, looking at a map of the route, go walking hither and thither all over the town in the footsteps of one of his characters. Without of course getting up to any of the lewdness as well.

Ah but there is in the nature of the Irish a deep fear of offending the poet and the dreamer man who can by his uttered or written word heap eternal scorn upon you and doesn't avoid doing the same upon any of your relations. And perhaps for that reason there haven't been more of your Irish kicking their authors in the teeth. Indeed there are plenty who secretly read and revere these rebels. And one recalls once walking along the main street of a provincial town and seeing high upon the front of a building a cement frieze which proclaimed for all citizens to see that it was The Literary Institute. And in the rainy chill of the evening you'd wrack your brain wondering to imagine who it was in years past who with a scruffy sheaf of paper under an arm might ever have been hanging around such a place with a serious novel, or a tragicomic stage play wrapped in a newspaper or a poem about rural life scribbled on a cigarette packet stuck in a pocket. And hoping that one day the contents of these pages might be revealed to the world. Or at least a copy secretly circulating and read by the local chemist, butcher, publican or newsagent. Without them later getting cudgels to give him a belt across the noggin or polishing their boot tips to give him a kick up the backside so as to be sending him out of town fast and take with him his dirty, disgusting insult to religion that would be masquerading as a drama, novel, poetry or play.

Now one of the things to know about this nation is that not everyone in the place writes. But don't expect very often to come across the few that don't. So there's no shortage let me tell you of pencils and pens scribbling and typewriter keys thumping the page. Nor by god is there any lack of descriptions these days that you wouldn't want your old maiden aunt to be reading by torch light under the bedclothes. And is it any wonder. In a land where solitary masturbation only half helps endure the rage against the repression and frustration, and where curtains twitch at every window, and where the small minded snigger and scoff and wag to spread gossip from ear to ear and door to door. Or where the scourging tongue can be upon you lashing to drive you out. And if that weren't enough then the grey skies and seeping damp rain, if they didn't drive you to drink certainly would inspire you to at least say something to defy such climatic elements. And why not be lewd about it as only words can be. For there is only one thing more distracting upon this earth than a graphic portrayal of a hearty fuck. And that is a soul inspired fuck itself. And that is another thing that has changed in the land of the shamrock, that you may as well be hung for doing it as be hung for describing it.

And now here we come full tilt to your Man Fighter Mark III. To confront her brains, beauty and wit. And by god all you small farmers and modest income tourists beware. Don't be getting ideas. She's not your cup of tea. And changing with her hair style, she's got big plans going way far into the future. With big colour photographs to reckon with her outspoken newspaper and magazine opinions, in which she supplies answers to the questions she's asked about her novels, poems, paintings and plays. Which give graphic descriptions of the foibles of your man who supported her through her first scribbling efforts, and even, by god, who often put his own paintbrush and pen to paper to help. And was she grateful? Not a bit of it. She instead branded him a monkish monster egotist. Now why, you'd ask, didn't he in the time honoured manner give her a good belt in the gob to put manners on her and then refuse to pay the dental bills to replace the teeth that had gone flying? Well now that's a good question. Probably best answered by the fact of your man being a gentleman and not wanting to go to prison where such an attribute would not be appreciated. Instead didn't he finally get her out of his hair by introducing her around to all your influential people, with her holding a shamrock and batting her eyes at them and opening her legs when the time for that was ripe. Sure and all the while your Mark III lady made it sound as if she had invented love. Posed there as she is once again demure in the newspaper, her countenance freeze framed suggesting her availability for seduction. Terrible, terrible, terrible, you might say. Well I'd say again, right back to you, not a bit of it. Why not. Isn't your Mark III a true Man Fighter, not mincing her words on the printed page and not afraid to call your man's horn a prick that would not only whip a donkey out of a sandpit but also lever a camel over a sand dune. And let me tell you, don't they know it's the women on top. And don't they know the mouse, the man, is underneath. Which brings us to the most successful, if not the most obvious, Man Fighter of them all, your Mark IV. Now this little lady by dint of her persistent nagging has silenced your man the husband into utter abject obedience and has him now sitting there on a bench in the pub as she points at him, with his hands folded in his lap and looking as if he'd passed beyond into another world. Which of course he has.

"Look at him, look at him. Didn't I bate him and bate him? It took years but there he is, not a peep out of him. And doing what he's told."

Ah but although your Man Fighter Mark III hasn't managed to quell her husband quite as well as your Mark IV variety, nevertheless as she moves at her ease about the artistic and literary world and is plamásing the men left right and centre, her flattery is getting her everywhere. Flicking up the tie of your man and telling him that not only is it long and hanging well but that she'd bet she could swing from it if it ever suddenly got rigid. And a true femme fatale you're saying. To be seen peering out from between the aspidistra leaves and in front of her captivated men heard waxing lyrical in her usual saccharine manner about frog spawn or the special sensual flesh colours she's mixed to paint her male nudes. And why not. Wouldn't the publisher and gallery owner be splashing the risqué remarks and her exotic stories of loose morals all over the public place. And then be up on his hind legs taking the bids for the book to be made into a film or the paintings to be exhibited in Paris. And then by god the saucy antics and romantic words in all their seductive octaves would then be coming at you in full colour off your worldwide screens and giving Ireland a name it would soon deserve. But never mind, if that's what it took to have the really big money coming in, sure it would be no worse than publicising your woman's brassière size and that would only be a number and the rest left to your imagination. And so not that much later your lady Man Fighter Mark III has got floodlit lawns around the house and Irish wolfhounds to bite the arse out of the curious trying to stare in her windows to witness herself flagrante in delicto with more than a man's tie that recently took her fancy. Of course the guard dogs would have the previous scent of the previous husband fucker who once drunkenly jeered at her at the typewriter and easel and who might sentimentally show up to do the same again. But then he'd be wasting his time. For hasn't her press agent issued a statement for immediate release that she's just departed solo to Italy and Spain. But he makes no mention that it is to have if off back and front with Latins. And in spite of an occasional venereal affliction and her passport and credit cards stolen, and the waiter with room service having an uninvited go at her, she otherwise had a grand old duce of a time. And don't worry, returning to the ould sod with a timely photograph in the newspaper and interviewed as to her recent opinions on the human female condition, she'd also

J . P . D O N L E A V Y

A SINGULAR COUNTRY

let you know you'll read more about her venereal adventures in the sizzlingly explicit pages of her next novel, or see it all writ nude in her next exhibition of paintings. And by god there need be no further hints dropped that little of it will be in your vernacular of vague shapes or innuendo.

Now from all of this previous you'd be getting a real slant on what this country is recently all about. On all media fronts outdoing the world in your lewd liberalism and your irreverent scatology. Able to do so since the few left of your upper cruster Anglos, who have intact their identities and previous symbols of domination, now go low profile about their business, leaving latitude in the example they set for a distinct and woeful lowering of standards. And there has been going around an oft heard national refrain "Since Our Own Have Taken Over". Which hasn't in fact totally happened all over as it were, and where it hasn't happened, it must be admitted that the people there are glad. But it has happened in more than your majority of this island. However that is not to say the country is to be taken as gone totally amorally wild with loose living women and the female journalists belting their typewriters publicising the fact. But sometimes this expression would give you the impression that the people were under the domination of themselves, your ordinary hoi polloi and busy voting a bunch of your gobshite wanking connivers down from the country into authority. Nothing could be further from the facts. For there has come upon the scene the astonishing phenomenon of the Protestant Catholic. Now no one is saying that the folk going under this description are rapidly solving every problem and are the sole upholders of decency on this small island but by god save for their presence you'd soon have more than your yobboes and louts swarming out of control all over the place. Now make no mistake here. Your Protestant Catholic is still your old practising papist Romanist, complete with fingers counting up and down their rosary beads, scapulars around their necks and clanking coins into church offering slots all over the country. In fact you wouldn't find any more devout a sample of your ultramontane. Ah but wait for it. You wouldn't be encountering any evasive shiftiness should a question of veracity arise. These would be to a man persons of exemplary character and unquestioned honesty who would have established widely known, long term, eminently respectable reputations. And who have now happily emerged conspicuous in their numbers upon the Irish scene. And they have many of them not only infiltrated in the law making and are powerful in the professions but have also contributed brilliantly to the running of such establishments as the Irish Country House Hotel and many more of your other thriving new businesses big and small across the land. And let me tell you they've given a big thumbs up for Ireland and may there be more power to them.

Now I know what you're hopefully thinking. You're thinking that for the sake of peace and quiet over the whole of the island, there would be in the converse such a thing as your Catholic Protestant. Ah may the Lord if he is alert above forgive you for so thinking. For you'd be wrong. Wrong. Wrong. And the answer would be. Never. Never. And not on your Nellie. And in other languages it would be Nyet and Nein. And if you'd still want the answer repeated in your incomprehensible Finnish and Hungarian, it is Ei and Nem respectively. Ah, you'd ask in your boyish and girlish innocence, why is that? Well for a start it would be long remembered history. And then on top of such unforgettable events and heaped high, had you a microscope powerful enough, you would see it plain as day written verbatim in your genetic code. But never mind history, or the double helixes demonstrating your hereditary blueprints. Or the fact that there is no such thing as the converse of this rapidly merging identity. Let's just be thankful that it's your Protestant Catholic who is the answer to all the social political and religious ills that do be besetting this land. And each day that goes by, thank the lord above, sees this exemplary sort of person pro-liferating against the vast tide of your vulgar hoi polloi. And setting new ethical and moral standards if not everywhere then at least here and there. And if at first you don't encounter them, whatever you do don't stop looking.

Now I know you'll be asking awkward questions as to how would you know one of this particular esteem if you saw one. Well for a start motor discreetly up to your nearest golf club. Enter. Even though this is your élitist sport of your upper cruster, you'll find your Irish golf club friendly enough. But as a non member do not announce your purpose of seeing for yourself a genuine Protestant Catholic. Because eyebrows raised they'll pretend immediately not to know what on earth you're talking about.

"I say there, could you possibly help me, I am looking to find a living specimen of what I believe is referred to as a Protestant Catholic."

"Ah sure no problem. And I suppose you'd be on your guard for a bogus example. Just wait there a second till your man is finished in the locker room changing out of his knickerbockers back into his clothes. Ah there goes one of them now, the genuine article, on his way into the bar."

Well I was wrong about that one. Clearly an exceptionally astute club manager. But back to the task at hand. Do not instantly expect for your man to stand out like the proverbial sore thumb, however, his tailoring as he passes you and heads to the club bar will invariably give him away. In a word, the cut of his jib will be well nigh impeccable. And those of you with good tailors will know whereof I speak. Now you may not have the opportunity to pass the time of day by returning something he has dropped but if you did be assured you would be rewarded by a ready smile and hearty handshake. He will meanwhile have exactly two gin and tonics while sitting by the lounge window looking out upon the green of the eighteenth hole. Now although your golf club will have more of your Protestant Catholics assembled at the one time than nearly anywhere do be alert, as the club manager suggested, for an impostor. So it is wise to know at least a mite more about the Protestant Catholic. They are sticklers in arising promptly of a morning and to lay down to bed of an evening long before midnight. They are deeply fond of household pets and especially their dogs whom they call by marvellously clever names and who would have a diet and schedule equal in nourishment and routine to their own. Their lawns are manicured upon which they slowly stroll. And they can be seen standing or sitting the contented hours away in their gardens anticipating the blossoming of their flowers. They go for bracing walks along Ireland's coastline, eschewing your more blatant American casual apparel which has recently hit this nation a fatal sartorial slap in the face. As you would imagine they would themselves wear your traditional tweeds and never be without a proper walking stick hand cut from the hedgerow. Now don't you all go rushing to see if you can see the man himself ingesting great lungfuls of the sea air. He'd be there all right but not in your obvious hoards. For a start he would choose a time of day early of a morning or evening to be as solitary as possible in pursuing his constitutional and would not demur or take shelter from rain or storm lashed gale. You guessed it. He's an outdoors man plain and simple.

Now another salient factor to remember concerning this elegant hybrid example of your present Irishman is he would ince like your most scalded cat from your nouveau riche pretensions of your present nauseating vulgar persons also to be regrettably found in the golf club and waltzing along the seashore and who boast of a lifestyle in which they order their champagne brought by the milkman. And advertise to anyone within earshot the well known brands of their cars, which they refer to by loudly mentioned nickname. Which leaves no doubt as to the kind and expense of vehicle to which they refer. Now although your genuine Protestant Catholic abhors these blatantly arriviste types, one must not get the notion that they are, as a new brand of Irish people, your staid old fusspot cranks faithfully saying novenas of a Friday evening and shoving their respectability in your face. Of for the matter of that, stuffing their gobs with compost-grown foods even though as a matter of fact they recently do. But then they don't flaunt an air of 'I am healthier than thou'. Nae, these folk are as ready as your next Irish person to have a mildly risqué joke or see the funny side of a not too desperate situation. But they do not tolerate your chancer, con man or cad or your reprobate member of the lower orders who makes a habit of lying, thieving, or munching and nibbling if not feasting off the public purse. Their style is to be possessed of a genteel considerateness and a fervent social conscience based on fair play for the underdog. In a word these evolved Irish Protestant Catholics are unique to today's Ireland. And with mothers and fathers begetting sons and daughters of such dutiful species they'll soon be more than a few. And if you don't want to ruin your eyesight or exhaust your patience searching for them or if you have no inclination to hang around a golf club

Just believe
That unbelievably
They're there and
Up the Republic.

ON THIS LONELY STRAND YOU'D KNOW FOR A
CERTAINTY BY THEIR STANCE THEY WERE
INTELLECTUALS NOT LOOKING FOR MOLLUSCS BUT
FOR ANY RANDOM TRUTH THAT MIGHT COME TO
THEIR ATTENTION.

VIII

And since they're here, this new brand of Protestant Catholic have found their way into substituting for that status once conferred on your squire up in the big house by the word 'gentleman'. These modern days in Ireland, however, you'd nearly ask what in the name of god is that. Well it would be your man who still has in him the sense of honour. And bejesus what is honour an Irishman would say. And here now straight into your ear with poetic indentation is the current capitalised definition.

HONOUR IS THAT QUALITY ONE CHERISHES,
KEEPS, PROCLAIMS AND EXEMPLIFIES
UNTIL SUCH TIME AS YOU ARE DAMN SURE
CERTAIN IT WOULD DO YOU NO BLOODY
DAMN GOOD TO KEEP, CHERISH,
PROCLAIM OR EXEMPLIFY IT
ANY LONGER.

A SINGULAR COUNTRY

Now the reason honour gets short shrift in the land of the shamrock is because the Irish as a people long occupied, subdued and dominated as they were by the foreigner, never had a sufficiently unleaky pot to piss in or could get their clogs long enough up out of the bog to display this quality of ethical high mindedness. Thus the term 'gentleman' becoming as it has long been, an expression regarded as advertising the sort of fool ripe to be fleeced of his money or goods. And even if a brilliantly disguised Irishman in such a delusion and alert to this drawback would set himself up with the trappings of a gentleman and squire he wouldn't be lasting the course I'm telling you, surrounded in a flash as he would be in such plenitude by conniving rogues reducing him naked to his socks and them left smelly with holes.

So in the age which has wrought the demise of your chivalrous status known as gentleman, let there be rejoicing that the gap left is being filled by your Protestant Catholic. This is not to say that your traditional gentleman cannot be found if looked for in the nether corners of the morning rooms of your better clubs, excluding the night variety, who try to specialise in such ranking of such class. But it is alas a fact that the numbers of these upper crusted folk once noted for their natural gallantry, high minded principles and elegance of behaviour, are now so rare as to be considered de minimis in Irish society. Notwithstanding that circumstance you might in the presence and environment of the horse be cajoled into believing that your previous persons of courtly magnanimity are still all over the place. And in particular are to be found prevalent at your stud farm, polo match, or conspicuous in the paddock at the race meeting. By god, you'd be badly misled. Separate the wheat from the chaff. Take no superior nonsense from those strutting about in their equine equipage and exhibiting characteristics historically associated on this island with nature's noblemen. And certain words are called for here in exacting from such booted and horsed folk their warrant and making bloody sure straight off that they are not your sham squire and fake.

"I say sir are you possessed of a reasonably substantial amount of land as a freeholder or are you masquerading with nothing more than your suburban front and back garden to boast of?"

But do in such questioning make allowance for your more modest and unaffected Protestant Catholic whom a lot of your discerning people will spot either mounted for the hunt or examining the alignment of his polo mallet before the match. Nor be put off the scent by his unprepossessing appearance in the midst of any of these clipped vowelled horsey impostors. And what the hell, occasionally one can be liberal here, and as ranking among your would be gentleman gentry include those who have arbours, ponds and glasshouses in their back gardens. Or indeed who have a few mature fruit and nut trees. For the advent of the Protestant Catholic hasn't come too soon for the sake of the ultimate betterment of this Isle. Even your Orangemen, who stand for no nonsense in these matters would have to admit subtly that he feels a mite easier these days as he travels golf club to golf club the length and breadth of the country and thoroughly enjoying the latest Gaelic contributions to freedom in that part of the land that holds the world's record for the banning of evil literature. He'd even be cocking his hat at your Man Fighters Mark I, II, and III. And of course your Orangeman would be doubly pleased to encounter your multi-orgasmic man loving vicar's daughter. On or off her horse. Or in or out of her Ferrari.

But in Ireland everything is opposite to the obvious. And the country itself is best described as a conspiracy among the populace. To achieve a confusion of image to the rest of the world. And in this, it must be admitted, that without in the least trying, they have succeeded admirably. Especially in giving a good impression to the outsider while keeping hidden qualities that might make him abhor you. Be that as it may, you'd still want to vaguely know what was happening all the way down the social ranks to your bootless and unhorsed and your largely materially dispossessed hoi polloi. Which latter, let me tell you, is your different cauldron of eels entirely. Notwithstanding the fact that the innate character of even your lowest of low orders of the purely Irish retain a peculiar and individualistically aristocratic quality. Mind you, it would be a quality peculiar enough and some of course would unkindly attribute it to an overblown sense of their own self importance they attach to having been born in the country of the shamrock in the first place, of parents just like themselves. And that they and their existence is unique. Now you might think this is a stupid assumption for them to make in the extreme in a world where others are so blessed. Well believe it or not they have a point. For there is nowhere else on earth where you can be where you'd think you weren't who you were or weren't where you were because you were there. Did you understand that? Now if you didn't, don't worry. But it is this slightly disorientated state of mind and place, and being isolated for so long from the vulgarity of the modern world, that has cultivated the Irish to enjoy the sight of one another which in turn has lead to the happy go lucky nature of the people. Such accumulated contentment and self assurance, real or imagined, has now at long last nearly put the Irish inferiority complex to rout which, regrettably, had, when the Irish leave Ireland, become over the generations a major part of the nature of being Irish. And instead it now accounts for the strange reason why on St. Patrick's day in the United States every inhabitant of every ethnic persuasion of that country is in his green tie and sporting his spray of shamrock and presenting himself to all and sundry as an Irishman. Even to being ready, some of them, to give you a quick fist in the gob if chided as an obvious Greek, Black, Oriental or Jew that he's prima facie an arrant impostor. Resulting finally, I'm telling you, in it's being dangerous business to being Irish in any guise whatsoever. Except as your forelock pulling bog trotter.

Now you would betimes in the homeland of the shamrock itself be forgiven for expressing an observation as to where can you see your real ordinary down to earth and less blessed Irishman who isn't still standing there at the door of his thatched cottage owning a bit of land and smoking his clay pipe and day dreaming as he looked over the hedgerow and down the road into the infinity. For you'd be concluding no doubt that they'd all packed their bags to disappear in the long accustomed stream of emigration. Well you'd nearly be half right and nearly half wrong. For as the new history of the land of the shamrock unfolds they have, a great big plethora of them, gone to the periphery of the conurbation. And now why would they do that. They'd do that because out there on those sprawling housing and council estates they'd have available to them a cheap rent and maybe a mortgage and have as a result a house in which to eat and sleep and not have the roof leak. And by god these boxy little abodes both sprawling and built towering on top of one another are erupting to beat the band all over the place. And it is here on these brand new laid down streets that these days resides nearly your majority of the nation, fully subsidised. And Ireland long being a location where the pigs and chickens were running loose all over the parlour, you'd wonder how the government can afford it. Well they can't. But in the true Irishness of the situation, they can. And impressive it is too and another example of the conspiracy active among the population to live free of charge in neat comfortable little houses with wonderful, not to say astonishing, social amenities including your white ceramic flushing bowls. And where the inmates instead of using the tub to store the turf and coal, as they had previously been long accustomed to doing, now immerse themselves to take your perfumed bubble baths while humming the national anthem. And more power to them you'd say.

But let me tell you, this humanity and kindness to these subsidised, less well heeled members of the population with the non leaking roof over their heads, hasn't improved some of their manners one bit. There'd still be among them plenty of your small minded bigots putting the tongue upon you in the land where bigotry reigns supreme. And still plenty of them of the sort who lurk at the cracks between the window curtain, and eye on everything that passes. And from behind a hand, as busy as ever spreading rumour and gossip ear to ear like wild fire. And if you were wandering by in any way decently, if not stylishly, attired, there would be grumbling remarks from doorsteps and glaring stares trying to bore their enmity into any who might look to be that little bit better than themselves. Now these are still your brand of people who might smile and plamás you as a stranger, but who would also try to make sure you do not stay too long so that you'd be getting to know what awful fuckers we really are. But then by god, there are your better people here too. Who were once your aspiring Protestant Catholic and who were even once successful in Irish life and whose children were growing up refined and who were butchers or other entrepreneurial businessmen who either slowly descended or were suddenly busted into bankruptcy. And now are relegated and given the four walls you get in the tall housing blocks or are put residing in a terrace of these sprawling estates. It is they who find they have been dropped into this other suspiciously mean sea of humanity who now lurk around them like piranha fish ready to rip and tear by ignominy and hostility the remaining life from them. However, those who knew better times at least become possessed of a roof over their heads and not a bad roof at that, under which there's running water and electrocuting electricity, all for a reasonable rent. And who would expect everything to smell of roses in the new Ireland. Or for that matter be looking too deeply into the gift horse's mouth.

Now remember Dublin was once such a place as was unequalled the world over for the squalor of its slums. Death and rats haunting the alleys and hallways. And the coffins would be aloft on shoulders and in and out of these tenements. But all save the memory is now swept away. Leaving the modern Ireland which has spawned a strangely humane socialism. Ruled over by the little emperors who nobly sit behind their desks as they officiate over the dispersal of cash. Ready for them and most of your little tricks perpetrated by those beneficiaries, busy perfecting schemes to cheat it. And occasionally the miscreants are reported and caught and punishment meted out. But it's very much a benign administration. While more and more of your torturing and incitement to greed comes beaming down out of the skies. Burning images into all these new growing up souls whose antecedents were dispossessed. Just as they are now dispossessed of the old Ireland, bad as it was. It might have nearly been better than the television screen now doing all the educating and preaching. That this or that product is good for you. And that the standard of life we're showing in our situation comedies with all our very own pots to piss in, is even better for you. And of course truth be told it is. It is. And aren't we eating the junk and wearing the styles to prove it. We are. We are. But now I'll tell you what really is an aesthetically crying shame. That will forever here on in, play havoc with a once starvingly poor but contentedly devout population. It is that religion has gone to the dogs.

And here we come now to the really big regret and the change that has hit this isle a cultural hammer blow in the haggis. With the population up and dancing all over the kip with your permissiveness. And of course in and among this lot will not only be found your British vicar's daughter aiding and abetting but also your local models and débutantes, who haven't a trace left of your previously admired chastity. Fish on Friday is gone. The Latin mass is gone. The roofs of the chapels and churches are leaking. And you'd wonder what has this got to do with culture. Or the Irish of today. Well I'll tell you. Picture this nation as it isn't any more but once was. As you pass on the road or

street in town or country, there would in many a window
be a candle glowing in front of an artefact of the sainted or
sanctified. Your clergy, and plenty of them, were conspicuous in their communities in their black vestments or
monkish robes. Your devout of the population were bless-
ing themselves hurrying along laneways and pavements,
nuns nodding at them as they went to attend upon vespers
or make their novenas. A grand pious god fearing sight.
And the atmosphere of the nation was the aesthetic better
for it. In these hallowed churchly places, the echoes of
organs playing. Choirs chanting and singing. In the solemn
memory of the dead and dying, the incense filling the
chapel air. Your confessional boxes with lines of sinners
waiting outside their shrouded mahogany confines. And
inside, were you to tune an eavesdropping ear, would be
buzzing alive with the telling of real genuine sins. Albeit of
an old fashioned passé quality and the like of which perhaps
would not have involved the fancy copulation your man
enacted with your vicar's multi-orgasmic daughter. But if it
had. You'd hear questions shot at you like bullets from a
machine gun.

"And was she, my son, on top?"

"She was father, and spinning."

"For the sin of impurity say five acts of contrition and
for fugacious and fancy fucking repeat the rosary a thousand times. And spin no more my son."

And lined along the pews on their knees, heads bowed
into their hands, the forgiven and repentant mumble their
penance. And now on this isle even the most heinous of
despicable deeds are hardly sins any more. The Protestant
churches stand deserted, jackdaws nesting in their belfries.
The nunneries and monasteries closed. And you'd even be

afraid to stop anyone in the street to ask them do they still believe in God or do they now put their trust in their T.V. If they didn't laugh at you, you'd be lucky if they didn't give you a good kick in the shins for reminding them of the Almighty above. And if you did get kicked and then gave them back a good slap in the face for their cheeky irreligiousness begorrah they'd have equally profane solicitors suing the living holy god fearing excreta out of you.

And here we come to the very latest new notion in the nation. Never mind the dying of religion. A new system of belief has been born. The zealous nature of which has no equal in any of your known religious persuasions. And the prayer that's prayed would be in the form of a writ flying all over the place. And landing to claim injury, indignity, loss, maim, distress and any heretofore negligence attached thereto. With your populace getting dizzy tripping on kerb stones, or pretending that a leg of theirs has been contused by the fender of a motor car. Or that in the supermarket a packet of soap powder has fallen over onto their finger. Or that didn't they lie unconscious an hour with a wad of gristle from a sausage caught in their windpipe. And by god now that they're back up and breathing again after a lot of bad dreams, they're on to the lawyer to commence the action for damages in a hurry. And coast to coast it's nearly like the automatic winning of a lottery with the temporarily maimed for the purpose, hobbling on crutches into court with headaches, and your transitory crossed eyes, or joints not working, ears not hearing or brains not thinking. With your man there in the witness box alternately scratching and tapping his cranium. As the judge cross examines.

"Are you actually suggesting to the court that you

cannot think any more, having been able to think prior to the alleged injury?"

"I am Your Honour. Me head's no longer reasoning right, Your Honour. Not only am I not able to count me cattle one at a time but I no longer know of a morning it's only one of me there plain as day looking in the mirror."

"But, if I may interpose here, you are able to count to one."

"Ah I am that Your Honour but I can't get past it to what I used to count to being two and three."

Now suing for substantial damages has done one thing anyway. Although not adding to the collective honesty of the population it has in a stroke created your very latest member of the leisure class. Who's able to stay abed till noon and to buy new houses, new cars and go strolling hither and thither like any squire gentleman of yore while enjoying to keep his neighbours burning in envy. But by god, don't be mistaken by the ash plant or the tweeds he's wearing or the big lungfuls of air he's ingesting along the seashore that he's your Protestant Catholic. He'd be instead your genuine chancer and a downright scheming cunning conniver. Out to take the insurance companies for every last penny he can get and do it by every trick of deception some of which aren't listed yet in the books. And I know what you're thinking. You're thinking that with the collapse of religion and disavowal of honour that the place is running wild with your slick citizen pulling the wool over every decent insurance company's eyes who hasn't yet been bankrupted. Ah but we can take some solace here, from the fact that with so many of your tricky customers about, they're not only getting in each other's way but also perpetrating their chicanery on each other. The big companies too, would be wise to the fraud. And they'd be more alert than anybody to the demise of religion and the resulting dishonest and unfair play towards the rich and powerful. Now, you'd ask, do these low type persons ever go and confess to their defrauding feloniousness? And whisper to the priest their dishonesty perpetrated upon the big company. They do not. For your man of religion would tell them to go straight back to the counter of the insurance office and make amends. With your sinner in the confessional raising his voice

What
You mean
Give the money back
Not on your nellie
Padre

ACROSS THIS SAND TIDES RISE AND EBB WASHING
DUBLIN'S SINS AWAY. AND WHERE SOULS HAVE
WALKED AND LEFT A LENIFYING LEGACY.

IX

Now after hearing of a few hiccups in the emergence of the Emerald Isle into the modern go ahead world, you'd wonder what else might go wrong with the nation and island as a whole. And indeed there is another little matter going on here on this terra firma that you may have recently heard about although it is as ancient as the place itself. It is that there is an enmity of identity displayed among some members of the population and they are betimes at each other's throats and providing a situation in which some of your most reasonable men remain unreasonable. Now with the scenery, the fresh air and open fields and plenty of room for everybody you'd say, why in god's name is that? Well for a start it's not in god's peaceful name but it would be clear and distinct as your colours black and white. However, in the matter of the circumstance to which we refer it is two other colours at your loggerheads, these hues being conspicuously green and orange.

A SINGULAR COUNTRY

For simplicity's sake it is best to bring into focus these separate tones of racial pigmentation and put names on both which in turn displays the clear existence of your Orange Man on one side and your Green Man on the other. And ne'er shall the twain meet. And not only that but some of them would do more than just bust each other's heads. Now dedicated observers who do be commenting on the matter would say that the root of the problem was tribal and then some would attest to its being religious and more would aver it was economic. And your Solomons among the bunch would say it was more than a little of all three of these things. Now there's already enough intellectual cats let loose among the scholarly pigeons to make the feathers fly with doctrines, theories and explanations without creating more heat than you'd find in your nuclear fission. But one or two things let me tell you are for certain. Primary among them is that this would be a real battle. And not some of your push and shove that some of your opposed factions in the backward nations get up to in the rest of the world. Which must at least mean one thing. Whoever is in the struggle waging it, seriously means it. And no matter what anyone suggests or says as a solution, seems able to simmer it down, at least up until yesterday. But luckily it has for the longest time now been less than a total blood bath. And some of your more pragmatic folk might say, isn't that the trouble. Especially as an Irishman will always see both sides of an argument provided it can result in a fight.

Ah but there are other aspects to enmity as there are to love. And you'd nearly think sometimes that your Green Man is in cahoots with your Orange Man. Both blowing pipes and fifes and beating drums marching through the streets. Throwing stones at each other and shouting you dirty Green or Orange bastard. And be that as it may. But by god what are you finding as you look deeper into matters. You are finding that your Orange Man, your lambeg drum beater and loyal to the British Crown is travelling on your Green Man's passport, the same that has got the harp stamped on it and has not got a single trace of adornment connected with the United Kingdom. And your Orange Man, taxed with the anomaly, would say he's only doing it for the convenience of the friendly international reputation such passport accords. But then you might take that as a complementary reason as to why you have your Green Man, in his droves, travelling to Britain itself, looking for jobs, not to mention abortions, and helping themselves generously to medical treatment and welfare. And indeed not a few of them even becoming your high and mighty celebrities and putting on the dog and acting your tender loving and comic talking Irishman and charming plenty all over the kingdom. And why not. And more publicity to them.

But, ah god, now is it any wonder that you'd be forgiven for thinking as one might have been previously suggesting that the conflict, hostility and hatred is all symbiotic acrimony. And that there be instead more of your aforementioned conspiracy among the populations to foster furore for the sake of an interested but befuddled world watching. While they are busy as they are in motor cars and lorries roaring back and forth across all divides and happy as can be getting whatever it was on either side that was better for them to get. And they'd both, Orange Man and Green Man alike, smile a pleased smile and shake a hearty handshake with each other over the bargain. And some to do this would even go by train which despite the tearing up of many a mile of track still remains one of the greatest things, aesthetically, emotionally and spiritually in the country. Now in speaking of the railroad you'd be wondering what this subject has got to do with religion or politics or with the price of war. Well the answer is plenty. For, in the form of a railway track, there is existing a singularity of connection between the two areas separating your majority of your Orange Man in the North from your Green Man in the South.

Now it should be no surprise to you that there would be somebody blowing the ruddy poor thing up. But the interesting situation here is you wouldn't be puzzling very long over who it might be. And you'd conclude right away it would be the Orange Man blasting it to kingdom come. In order to keep the association of North and South to a maximum minimum. And you'd be wrong. And in the right answer might set the greatest example yet in the list of evidence of the conspiracy among this entire island population. It is your Green Man doing this frequent and now traditional job. Stuffing the explosive under railway bridges or between the ties on the track and waiting for the big locomotive pulling its fairly attractive train. Now the question must be still bedevilling you. As to why your Green Man is causing this impassibility and doing it maybe not always as regular as on every Wednesday, but nearly. And you'd get to the bottom of it by realizing that in more historic times this train was called the "Contraceptive Express" named after the then purpose of many of your Green Man travellers carrying these pregnancy-preventing artefacts from an area where they be legally available to one where they weren't. Now even in your less permissive times when this train was blown up, your Green Man did a great job of it. Not only did the detonation contort the rails of the track but it also sent your condoms flying, not as balloons but as a bunch of ragged shattered rubber bands. But if you were sitting innocent as your steady peaceful traveller on such a train, such explosions would exasperate you and you wouldn't exactly be concerned as to whether it was all for a good cause or not. But now here at last one knows why there is no contradiction in your Orange Man not doing the blowing up. For it is your Green Man who, in intercepting the traffic in your birth preventatives, would be aiding and abetting the increase in the population of the likes of himself. Making sure that he doesn't, as the Orange Man has done in the Green Man's part of the isle, disappear from sight.

Ah but an indisputably more important matter, and while we're on the subject, is not ever to let the Irish railroad disappear from sight. For, not the least of this amenity is your marvellous workforce who faithfully administer on these click clacking rails which still cross over many a peaceful mile of this island. Conductors, station masters, porters, ticket sellers, who are all men of astonishing depths of sensitivity, philosophical awareness and each with a propensity for matters droll. Now you're not for a second to deduce from this that they would be having a huge joke on the public and were broadcasting the wrong timetable or were sending trains in the wrong direction on the wrong rails or, worse, derailing them altogether. On the contrary where such confronts in their daily duties these dedicated men put everything right in what is commonly referred to as a jiffy. Humanity with a strange gentleness abounds everywhere among these gentlemen who will have seen in their time, a lot of punching of billets up and down the train. And although always with a wary eye out for fare evaders who might try hiding in the lavatory or proffering their out of date tickets, they are prepared to be lenient, understanding and kind. If the sound of your feet is approaching they will keep a train waiting till you safely board. Rarely do you find surliness where you have to pop someone on the kisser or slam someone a few kicks in the shins and anonymously rush away in the crowds. And not that this should make much of a desperate difference to you, but the width of the rail gauge is one of the widest if not the widest in existence. Which does at least guarantee to keep the train on the track and never mind the extreme occasion when a carriage or diesel locomotive is to be seen toppled on its side along the line. Unlike other busier railroads in the world, such an event hardly ever happens. And safely inside the carriage you'll be reassured by the smile these conductors wear and which is never far from their lips. For they have a lifetime of experience of the human predicament and when you are searching for your ticket which you cannot find, even tugging about in your underwear, they know the true from the false impression that this can give and recognising the genuine case, will even insist that you be given time to go on searching and undressing in the lavatory even when you yourself are already totally convinced you've lost your billet. But the indulgent conductor knows by the cut of your jib that you haven't. And that you've tucked it somewhere so that you would be sure not to lose it and sure enough when you've eventually calmed down from hysterically turning out your pockets and investigating the final nook and cranny of your top coat, and then at last in your underdrawers revealed in the lavatory, presto there it is to be presented when your conductor returns knowing with a smile that you'll have finally found it.

"Ah now didn't I tell you sir, to go on looking, recognising in your honest face, a careful kind of person not likely to lose your ticket and putting it into too safe a place to be found as it were."

Now it is not strange that on this wonderful rail network they do not make announcements in Irish. Not because it is believed by those in authority that there is confusion enough, but because most travelling the trains in the Emerald Isle already understand the language, and you wouldn't be telling them something they didn't know. And this brings us to another form of rapidly becoming popular travel and that be in the sky. Where, on the native powered flight, they do be announcing in Gaelic prior to take off for an Irish destination. Now no wonder heart attacks are increasing as well as causing Orange Men to exhibit pained distaste. However, there is another action more extreme and resembling that of the scalded cat. And this is your opportunity to witness a searing example of this as an expression when it appears on some of your foreigners' faces as they hear the first indecipherable syllables of the Erse language coming at them over the tannoy. With your less sophisticated Americans especially leaping half out of their seats at this sound, with husbands grabbing their wives' hands.

"Hey gee Mabel, what the hell's that? We gotta get off, honey. We're on the damn wrong plane to Timbuktu or somewhere."

Of course Irish speaking stewardesses on the national airline have long been trained to be able to calm such passengers who might be tempted to make a beeline for an emergency exit hatch waving their tickets and pulling down hand luggage on other passengers' heads. And decipherable languages are now speedily made to follow the native tongue announcements before passengers erupt to do anything foolish. Even so, with some local menus printed in Irish, there are still your Americans who with too much, or not enough, drink have been known to panic at hotel dining room tables.

"Holy cow Mabel this isn't even in French. How the hell are we going to know what we're eating when we don't know what we're ordering."

And so it is with this imaginative nation playing their little humoursome tricks on the visiting foreigner and tourist. And it would be in the form of a strange sublimation that has been stimulated over the centuries by your landlord domination and the steadfast belief in British tyranny. Plus given that every Irishman has a deep abiding faith in his own shrewdness sharpened over the year by the boggy if not rocky terrain. And now adding to the conspiracy of contradictions to be found everywhere in the land, your stranger and tourist would be in for some more of your shocks. And especially the one revealing the British and Irish secret love and admiration for one another which has been so long and carefully hidden from the outside world. Of course to your distanced alien watching his T.V. and reading his newspaper in faraway lands this is dreadfully confusing news to suddenly let out. Indeed if openly and widely admitted by these two, traditionally, supposedly opposed races who heretofore have been so discreet and secretive about the matter, it could suddenly produce boat and planeloads of your respective British and Irish spanning the divide of the Irish Sea. And arriving on each other's shores stepping on each other's toes as they throw arms around one another to embrace. While your Orange Man rushes to witness the unbelievable spectacle and to either stand by in fist shaking rage or else solemnly weep over such sacrilege. And your disbelieving American tourist, Harry is ready with his camera.

"Hey gee Mabel look at that. I gotta get a picture of this. These people really love each other."

Ah but do they, these people Orange and Green, really love each other. And perhaps no one will ever know. For again there is this constant mischievous intrigue among the population, which if you are foolish enough to bother to investigate, will produce all sorts of mistaken impressions. But let us take a rare example of what you would think couldn't prevail. And that is the astonishing phenomenon of the existence of your neutral Orange Man. Ah I knew you wouldn't believe it. But listen to this, here is a man who is as fair as you can get. Indeed, to whom even both sides of the difficulty would repair in order to mediate between the combatants. A gentleman of some elegance and verve, who is your moderate of no partisan leanings, a man independent, impartial, unprejudiced, unbiased, balanced. Who would see both sides of the question fairly and objectively and give Solomon's opinion in any kind of Orange versus Green circumstance you could mention. Ah, but if you put him out of the Irish cauldron of contention and into what one can fairly term is the neutral territory of indifference. Say, in the marvellous surrounds of an old luxury London hotel, ah god, where he now sits in his well tailored suit and tasteful silk tie and stretched back on the sofa pillows, as he gently tastes his gently bubbling glass of champagne which has just been served by one of the gently smiling liveried waiters. And at precisely this solemnly seven p.m. of an evening, under the glinting chandeliers, the assembled Hungarian orchestra prime their instruments and strike up appropriately with the tune of "O Danny Boy". When down from their suites above, the dowagers glittering in their diamonds, begin to gather as other ladies in their finery, and more recently of the world, waltz in. Taking their seats to study the menu over their drinks before dinner. And ah god, not far away, your neutral moderate non partisan Orange Man who is independent, impartial, unprejudiced, balanced and unbiased, and who would agree that it is only fair enough your Green Man would want to join your Orange Man in a oneness of a whole Irish nation, languishingly leans back in his chair and breathes in a great lungful of the luxurious British ethereal elixir. As he sighs in his ecstasy and is heard to intone.

"Ah. You know. The Empire and what we stand for and believe in must not be allowed to disappear."

And by god, would you believe it. The waiters, overhearing and listening, are to a man all Green Men, and in their fine livery are direct from the old Gaelic country west across the Irish Sea. And now hearing your neutral Orange Man's remark, you'd be sensibly ready to leap back like a scalded cat from the threatening imbroglio. But by god you'd be in for even a greater shock. Don't your liveried Green Men waiters instead bend even deeper in their bows and smile even wider across their Celtic faces and rejoin your Orange Man with a rejoinder of the deepest abiding understanding.

"Ah now sire in regard to your recent acoustics expressing that sentiment, don't we agree with you right down to the very last syllable."

The chandelier glistens its rainbow of colours. The marble pillars of this great lounge gleam. The dowagers peruse amid the entrées. And doesn't your Orange Man lean back a mite further in his sofa chair in sheer relishment at these words. And beams a smile back up at your two Green Men that would blind you by its very brilliance. And doesn't he now take another great sigh of pleasure and give a tiny discreet tug at his long silk black socks as he tunes his vocal cords to reply.

"Ah Paddy and Micko good men yourselves thank you for your welcoming concurring diphthongs. We all know well, don't we, that Britain is better for both of us."

"Sir, you can bet all your consonants that we do."

And with such understanding words spoken between your Orange and Green Man, why wouldn't your obstinate fanatical bigotry reign supreme. Especially as what is said between Irishmen, which between Irishmen, is meant never to wound or offend until such time as wounding or offending is necessary. And is it any wonder that the Shamrock Isle is the only country in the world where language doesn't mean anything. And if it did you'd only be repeating what you said yesterday, last week, last month, or last year or the year before that. And that's why you see all over the place everywhere you go, a sign language expressed in nods, gestures, beckonings, wiggles, salutes, winks, eyebrow and shoulder raising and nudges.

And they
Don't mean
Anything
Either

BRAVING THE CHILL DISCOMFORT FOR THE SAKE OF
GOOD HEALTH AND PLUNGING INTO THESE
FREEZING WATERS FOR A RESTORATIVE SEA SWIM
HAS BEEN A TRADITIONAL IRISH PURSUIT MOSTLY
FOR GENTLEMEN AND OFTEN IN THE NUDE.

X

Ah you're saying if there's no meaning in the language and if spouting incomprehensible Gaelic to innocent persons as Irish motor birds take off for the Emerald Isle at airports is giving the likes of old Harry and Mabel circulatory fribulations and threatened heart attacks, then you're saying what therefore does mean something in Erseland? Well I'll tell you. And by god it is listened to and read with eagerly awaiting ears and eyes. Gossip means something. And rumour. Plots and conspiracy and speaking ill behind the back. Which when it is translated into libel and slander means even more. For only in Ireland is a lie regarded as the truth told for the time being. But the falsehood meanwhile is meant to do as much damage as it can while it lasts as the truth. So you'd soon grow dizzy and flop down with exhaustion looking for candour around the place. And it would be an isolated incident indeed that you'd ever encounter the sort of defamation of the character that would erupt concerning say a restaurant, where old Harry might jump up like a scalded cat shouting over his vichyssoise.

"Holy gee Mabel there's a god almighty live snail with two periscope eyes swimming across my soup."

No need for panic here. All forms of Irish domiciled molluscs and crustaceans are of the very purest, best and highest quality and deservedly desired by your best gour- mets from Paris to Timbuktu. And of course any of your normal Irishmen in the purlieus would be only too delighted to snatch up, raise high and drop into his mouth this fresh live snail paddling in his soup. However old Harry from Dayton, Ohio, hysterically all over the place hollering, has hit this upmarket hotel restaurant a real hard if not low blow in the old haggis. And due to the mouth to mouth communication system across the country this is not a place where you can shout out or for long talk behind somebody's back without them soon having wind of it. And never mind your telephone, telegraph, morse code and facsimile systems. They're not needed. For in a land where everyone wants to get something for nothing and where begrudgement lurks supreme and vilification is the highest of all arts, the Irish are, like Harry, wont to say anything they can constructively destructive. And here by god does the language more than occasionally mean some- thing in communication. Especially if it is maliciously libellous and defamatory and someone is suing the living bejesus out of you for having brought them into ridicule and contempt and hoping to reduce you down to your broken shoelaces in bankruptcy. And Dayton Harry might soon find writs instead of snails in his soup. So in your innocent excursions in and about this island you'd always want to have a mind to please and be flattering in the conduct of your social intercourse with your hail fellow well met Irishman. And in the case such as Harry's he'd have better been advised to aver.

"Hey gee Mabel look at this little live bonus they give you here to garnish your soup."

For let me tell not only you this, but Harry and Mabel as well. That by joining this time honoured conspiracy among the natives and giving out the blarney and bathing your words in complimentary overtones, such will bade you better than well. And there's even a Gaelic word for it, plamás. Which, in its English language definition is the laying on thick of flattery. With maybe an overtone of soft soaping and wheedling thrown in. And this would get you peacefully and pleasurably from Ballinamuck to Ballybofey and back in no disagreeable time at all.

Now as you'd not too innocently imagine there's a bloody good reason lurking in this velvety benign behaviour. For libel cases frequently threaten and often finally rage in this land where ridicule and contempt have long been honed into a fine art and have been a recognised method of getting even with them as you have no use for and who in fact you'd like to see dead and as indecently buried as possible. And this kind of rancorous litigation has no resemblance to the previous popular type mentioned involved in falling off trams, trains, buses or tripping over paving stones. Or the near miss in a motor car brushing past someone's limb which, after you stop out of courtesy, then by god produces an army of fifty accomplice witnesses shouting that you've cracked two and bruised four of your man's best ribs, dislocated his spinal cord, put the cartilage in both knees on the blink and twisted his coccyx back to front. And don't worry, although your man will then be hobbling on crutches into court, his ears held up by balloons, having conferred with his solicitor, it won't be long following the collected award for the damage and maim that he isn't back the next day from Lourdes miraculously cured and tap dancing all over the place. And it would have your fair minded honest Protestant Catholic protesting.

"Shame. Shame. Shame."

Ah but we were talking instead about defamation and injury to the reputation and the monetary awards of indemnification arriving therefrom. And if you or your lawyer have enough shekels to afford the first day in court, by god if this isn't a great old game going on. And never mind the use of language here, the protagonists in this courtroom battle will be killing each other with looks. And with the intensity of enmity blazing down these laser beams, in a few glances there'd be no one alive within miles. Nor would it take you long to be quickly wondering what to do to avoid this kind of prolonged implacable human consternation. And it would be no surprise to anybody if you from now on, instead of complaint, settled for plamás. And in the restaurant, viewing your dreadful cold sodden greasy overcooked meal, and an earwig running at you out of the cabbage and even trying to get up your sleeve, to confound the head waiter into making it sound as if you were delighted by the sign of living nature under your very nose which amply demonstrated the healthy condition of Irish earwigs. For the proprietor now would be summoned fulminating from the back and beyond of the kitchens, in order that he might be ferreting around in every syllable you utter to make sure he's got the nuance of the maliciousness that could mean the very worst defamation or slander that could give vent for revenge suggested in the law books. Ah, but the earwig has now rushed into the dark safety under the edge of your plate and you're ready as your man bends to ask,

"Is everything to your satisfaction sir?"

"Ah god these do be great peas and potatoes served by a great waiter. And there not be a sign of any old cooked dead bugs, rottenness or blemish anywhere and the whole lot is delicious."

Now employing the English language in its Irish vernacular is another of your communicating helps the visitor is wise to adopt and to which Dayton Harry has caught on and is now finding is smoothing his path through Ireland. And indeed putting on the brogue has long been an art in conversation used by your ruling Anglo Irish ascendancy landlord in speaking and dealing with your native estate and household staff. With the pasha in the big house taking his ease reading the newspaper while toasting his toes before the library fire and having his pre dinner sherry.

"Would you ever Paddy now be after getting in a few more sods of turf to be keeping the flames leaping and the heat hopping on the hearth?"

"Sure your Honour and that's something now sire that I'd only be too glad sir to be attending to this very moment."

One can think of a few rude ripostes, that might underlie these words from Paddy here, and be assured of course that he won't be tiring himself getting any old turf until the fire has gone out. And the pasha has frozen his upper cruster balls off and had to smash back five more sherries to kill the chill. But all indeed is fully in keeping with the Country House tradition in which efficiency and dutifulness are instantly promised and inefficiency and insubordination are then leisurely perpetrated. As too, in the same way on the Shamrock Isle, friendship, although on the lips, is but a thin disguise of the betrayal lurking in the heart. And those you thought were cheerful acquaintances easily convert without warning into bitter enemies and adversaries. And so as the libel case unfolds in the courtroom you'll be thanking your lucky stars you were smart enough not ever to have put pen to paper or tap a computer or typewriter key, or sign a guest book, because let me tell you that even the disapproving frown you were seen wearing on your face five years ago at two in the afternoon will be remembered and thoroughly used against you.

"The expression on his face Your Honour, would kill a cat. And him black with nine lives."

But by god never mind court decisions, revolutions, or earthquakes. For in the world's friendliest country, even worse than litigation befalls in the matter of a slight snub, the Irish memory for which is the longest in Christendom. Indeed this is why anyone walking a street in Erseland is, if he isn't walking backwards or sidewards, forever nodding on all sides of him. And many a nut, taking pleasant acknowledgement of another to an extreme, sports clerical garb and sprinkles holy water in all directions. But of all disparagement and belittling, being ignored is the most heinous, and goes forever unforgotten and unforgiven down the generations and centuries. With the treasured moment for getting even always as much cherished as it is constantly visualised and faithfully awaited.

Now you'd think from what's been said there would be

a bit of caution in your snubbing and the use of rumour and gossip. And that there would be utter fear and trembling everywhere to in the least, or by any means, offend anyone. But not a bit of it. Nothing could be further from the truth. Not only does bitter bad mouthing and smearing aspersion go criss crossing the country from lips to lips but poison pen letters not necessarily anonymous flood all over the kip through the post with no one hesitating to put pen to paper to spell out the scurrility, even to communicating to those abroad. Although it is admitted however, that when blatantly putting these maliciously defaming and libellous matters in writing such communications are always headed in capitals.

BURN THIS LETTER IMMEDIATELY AFTER
IT IS READ.

Of course already eagerly handing it hand to hand, and often intoning the contents aloud nobody ever burns anything containing so much juicy heartfelt gossip. Even sexual positions and proclivities are carefully calculated to be as disgustingly disparaging as possible and are often briefly encapsulated so to brand their victim with a nickname forever. And these are especially vituperative in belittling or besmirching a lady's reputation especially when referring to depraved and corrupt moral behaviour as might be involved in spinning like a top with your multi-orgasmic vicar's daughter whose Ferrari the Irish female assemblage battered to an unsalvable wreck.

Now is it any wonder that you have libel actions erupting at the drop of a hat all over the kip. And if you were ever stupid enough to say anything in your own handwriting anywhere, bejesus it could rear up any time now in volcanic conspicuousness. The writs flying with counter accusing solicitors' letters questioning the parentage and slanging words back and forth alluding to the past bad character of the plaintiff and deserving of the present defamatory remarks. Ah but there is a world in Ireland where there is no litigation. But much fornication. And your Irish natives are wont to be even more flamboyant in their phrasing to describe your female of morals loose. And by god isn't the province we refer to that of fox hunting.

"Wasn't she now mounted or dismounted a fuck laid on like hot water in the pipes and them tingling with the heat and couldn't anyone come cantering along and turn on the tap."

And in these galloping hunting circles so bad has the general gossip got that you'd these recent years even have members of the clergy involved. Ah but more anon about matters of the horse, fox and hounds. But before we forget all this old slander and scandal stuff you'd wonder what was the worst that can be said about someone aside from his being branded an ignorant bollocks. Which latter, in an island proud of the education of its inhabitants, is usually the first loud aspersion cast. And be that as it may. But in a land where the people are generous to a fault the most demeaning comment is simply that your ignorant bollocks is not only an ignorant bollocks, but is mean and stingy as well. And wouldn't buy a thirsty man a drink.

And him
Just awake
From a dream
Midway across the
Sahara desert

THIS NOBLE FORM OF TRUSTY TRANSPORT ONCE
SO FAITHFUL AND BELOVED HAS NEARLY VANISHED
FROM THE CITY. BUT THERE DO STILL BE THOSE
INTREPID WHO PEDAL ON.

XI

Ah but with all its asses and carts, greeny brown moun-
tains and silver streams, golden thatched cottages and lonely
bogs and plethora of pubs, here you are alive in Ireland
ready to enjoy what this country offers more than anywhere
else in the world, the opportunity for the mind to dream.
Always provided of course such imaginings are of a pure
and chaste nature. Then let us suppose as an unabstracted
stranger and visitor plamásing all around you and libelling
no one, that you'd have had no trouble, and been giving
out the blarney as good as you've got and that on wheels
without a horse you're trying to only be doing the simple
enough thing of heading where you want to go. Well you'd
soon be in a dilemma and be warming up your brogue to
utter a stream of your Irish vernacular profane expletives.
For disorientation of the foreigner is the greatest game
ever played by any of your indigenous natives anywhere.
And you wouldn't in a hurry be finding the way to

Twomileborris or Ballyboggan especially if you had like poor old Harry from Dayton, Ohio, the unluckiness to accost one of your passing rural rustics to enquire the way.

"Ah now you're not that near that it could be said you're not that far away. And again now you're not that far away that I couldn't tell you how to get there."

"Well gee, fella thanks, how do you get there?"

"Now stay aboard your motorised vehicle and continue to roll on down this road till you meet the fork going right and left where you'll see straight ahead of you a bush standing so high next to a tree. It would be a perennial of a type better known on the slopes of the Gulf of Genoa and brought back here to these parts of the world by the one time local lord of the manor from over there beyond who shot himself through the head in his library while reading the order for the burial of the dead from the book of common prayer according to the use of the United Church of England and Ireland. Wasn't your man's butler outside the door listening before the shot rang out. And his lordship had on great funeral. But let's never mind that old bit of history. You'd be wanting I'm sure to be on your way. But back to that bush now, if it had been warm enough this past spring the bit of shrubbery planted by your lordship would have yellow flowers on it as big as the size of half a crown with a harp on one side and a stallion on the other and that no longer would these recent times be legal currency, having gone out of circulation these five or was it six years ago and a pity it was too. With your commissars in power having no regard for the historic nobility incarnate in the nation's coinage. And sure it would be just like a lot of other things the powers that be have let go to the devil."

"Gee fella, sorry you sort of got a problem here. But that bush you mentioned a while ago."

"Ah of course. The bush. Wasn't I just coming to that. Well now you can't miss it and you'll recognise it even with the flowers. But take no notice of it. It should have been pulled up out of the way years ago. A danger to road users it would be, who'd bechance know and be distracted by its rarity."

"Holy cow fella, what do you say we sort of skip the shrubbery a second. And maybe just tell us which way to go."

Now all this palaver by your local native with Harry and Mabel as a captive audience who are desperate to get the hell on their way, is for no other reason than to simply hold as lengthy as possible a conversation. The rustic himself doing all the talking. For it would only be with the passing alien stranger that your aboriginal could ever get the wee chance to spout out his timeworn brainful of clichés and platitudes that would be long familiar already with every member of your local populace who for miles around have over the years heard your man repeat ad nauseam his twice told tales a thousand times. But even so, Dayton Ohio Harry, in attempting to get himself faster to where he was going, would be entirely much wiser to straight off suggest repairing with your homegrown road-side rustic to the nearest pub and while repeatedly buying him foaming dark pints of stout, tune in his ears to your man for the night. For let me tell you where ever you're headed and reading the road signs or listening to another colloquialist pointing the way, you'll never get there. Since every destination put up printed to be bilingually read, if the understandable language is not torn in half, then what's left of the sign will be twisted in the wrong direction. And why not, if one is in mind of the fact that the whole place is not that big an island and a quick walker could non stop cross it in two days and that you would come to the coastline and a cliff edge or beach before you would be totally lost. Plus you would of course, provided it's still daylight, be getting a great old mystery tour, that would be revealing to you many a great sight that you would be sure to miss if you weren't lost. So in fact it couldn't matter less, not knowing where the bloody hell you're going. But giving wrong bearings as the national pastime is for more heartfelt reasons than amusement alone. And that is because some of your sleek obtuse foreign tourist excursionists looking down their noses at the poor primitive roadside native, bloody well deserve it.

Now for a decent moment if you will, picture how you would feel if you were the descended from the famine shambling old rustic himself standing there lonely and forlorn on this god forsaken road, holes in your every pocket as you reached fiddling to adjust your stale old goolies as they become misplaced for the hundredth time in your tattered uncomfortable mouldy underwear. With socks on unchanged for weeks that would stand up and walk by themselves. And you'd be itchy enough wherever there was a patch of hair growing on you and off which even if you took only the mildest sniff, nothing would come let me tell you, that would even remotely be as naturally perfumed as new mown hay. And now suddenly out of the greeny blue distance on this ghostly haunted, deserted road, appears a grand shiny new motor car driven by your talcum powdered, toilet lotioned leisurely dressed tourist. Cameras and assorted lenses slung gleaming around their necks. The wife sporting a wristload of gold bracelet charms plus glittering, gaudy assorted plumes, garlands and spangles galore that would, were your aboriginal able to get his hands on them and put them into pawn, buy him meals and drinks for months at a clip. Sure just to peek into the back seat of the automobile and feast your eye on the stack of the best of top grain, cowhide luggage, you'd know the pair of them had money to burn. As what else could be the situation with people with nothing better to do than to be wandering around one of the loneliest landscapes in Europe as strangers. And then by god here you are the genuine bogman himself, the still moist cow flop on your heels putting your best boot forward and forelock pulling to eagerly take any and all trouble to give them the best account you can of the local folklore liberally embellished with precious items of interest not to be found in any guidebook. And there they are, indifferent as you please, the smug sweet smelling impatient pair of them ungratefully on the verge of wanting to tell you to shut up, you old god damn boring tramp. All they care about is just simply the directions to get the hell away from you as fast and as far as possible. And by god is it any wonder that as they finally roar off in a blaze of exhaust and tyres scorching the road, that you, scratching to relieve the itching in your goolies, have sent them, as best as you know how, miles in the continuously circular wrong direction. And also with the fervent bon voyage wish that the pooka would have pissed aplenty upon the blackberries they might have served up for their evening's dessert if ever by an absolute miracle they get to where they innocently think they're going. Instead of to the endlessly elliptical place you've sent them. And if you don't know who the pooka is, don't worry, he'd only be here lurking in Ireland where if you come he'd be enlightening you soon.

But now you heard your man the rural rustic mention the word 'horse' more than once. And it would be in this misdirected situation of not knowing where you're going where such an animal beats wheels any day. Unless of course you don't straight off plummet down into a ditch or get flipped frontal somersaulted on your neck over a wall and get your ass broken. Or end up horse's arse deep in a bog. Or like any arrow get shot head first into a meadow when your steed puts a hoof in a rabbit hole and you get incarcerated indefinitely in hospital. Now it is well known that Irishmen are not great lovers of animals, unless they are making him money. And there would not be jams on the telephone lines reporting complaints to the Society for the Prevention of Cruelty to Animals. And plenty of your folk would as soon kick a dog in the face if they knew it wouldn't bite their foot off. Ah but as with a poor farmer's petted cow it would be different. Mollycoddling would be the order of the day. And the same would apply to a horse that in a meadow would make the grass look greener, and if the nag was at all presentable with ribs covered with flesh and no conspicuously dipping in the back or too much slopping in the quarters, such an animal would raise the status of its owner. For the horse, evident all over this country, is the national symbol. And to race, jump, groom, pet or bet on it, is approved by all. But if you want to mount or ride on its back you'd be that bit more better than you'd be just standing holding your horse's halter. And you'd improve one better even than that if you were in your snood, stock, booted leather and hard or silk top hat, to play polo, race or hunt it. Flying over the ground, side saddle or your horse within your bifurcation. Plus by god, keep the gallop going and before long you'd excel to the stratospheric. And you'd know soon too, why in Ireland, if a great jockey enters a chamber, all the assembled to a man stand as they would in Britain for your top royalty or in America for the President himself.

Now don't all rush at once to your tailor and boot-maker to equip to jump into an Irish saddle. But if you added to your regalia a pink coat on your back and gave chase to the fox you'd then be known as arrived, yourself among very upper crusters where you'd be operating under the biggest mystique of all. For the snobberies attached to the pursuit of this country pastime of fox hunting and trying to catch this cunning and elusive devil, are immense. For a start there's no single section of people in this world who think more of themselves and less of others. And by god when fitted out in their kit and up on their mounts and ready for the tracking down of this canine, never mind your ignored old rustic giving out his well meant information with his directions to the American tourists on the side of the road. This lot would, as you stood there beneath them on the ground, look down at you, look through you and look away from you. And then by god let the fox appear and the huntsman sound his horn. They'd pay plenty of attention then. To gallop off and ride over you as if you weren't there. And it's not because they've just spied the fox lurking along the hedgerow, it's because they think you are bloody well not worth knowing. And they go with others of their ilk, till the hounds track down this canine and leave nothing but a bit of steam rising from the grass where the russet haired poor creature was last seen to stand his ground and emit a final growl and snarl.

J . P . D O N L E A V Y

A SINGULAR COUNTRY

But let us say now that you'd like on the Shamrock Isle
to improve yourself and become one of them and sit up
there all decked out superior and as Anglo Irish as possible
on your high horse. Well you'd get a shock. For if you are
new to the sport there is in the first place no way that you
could appear in the field as anything other than the rank
out and out novice and no doubt social climber that you
are, standing out like the biggest of all big sore thumbs in
Christendom. Of course foolishly trying to make an impression you'd have already acquired the best looking steed and
been to the best booters, reputable tailors and hatters, and
with bills to match that would make most folk faint. And
in this attempting to look your impeccable best and giving
what you would guess was no possible offence to the other
long term members of the hunt, you'd find you'd still be
taken aside to be reprimanded by those in seniority and
your presumed betters for having the audacity to appear
impeccable. This of course only heightens your intention to
ride these pretentious bloody pomposities into the ground
at the first cry of "Tally ho". But now too let us assume
you not only have amended your sartorial ways to avoid any
but the lightest of criticism and you were keeping your
place, you'd still be as it were in the firing line for even
worse tongue lashing and cursing ridicule. Some of which is
quite brutally direct.

"I say, damn you, you arrant impostor, get you and your
fucking horse out of my way."

Now this is all very Irish indeed. But count yourself
lucky that whips are not lashing you across the face. And to
avoid such verbal opprobrium and vilification on a hunt
you'd need to go straight home or ride to hide somewhere
fast well away from the line of the fox. And of course as

nature would have it, this is always exactly where this Celtic canine is going too. And then suddenly there both of you are. The dear old pretty fox peeking out from the edge of the glade and gently looking up enquiringly at you as you sit there in the middle of your saddle, tears seeping down your face. Because those old mean hunt members have been dreadfully rude to you. Now why do people with so much of this kind of personal sorrow befalling them do this chasing of the fox at all, you're asking. Well for a start, in a very acceptable upper cruster way, it enables you in the otherwise free and easy society of Ireland, to bring out and exhibit your killer instinct while at the same time risking your own and your horse's neck which proves your nerve and lack of lily-liveredness. But there's more. And to quote from the very folk themselves, it's how to associate yourself with the right people. Which, especially in Ireland, would straight off be those who can afford your kit, the tack and the horse. And then the stabling, the grass, and the hay with which to feed them. Followed by the generous sized thick woolly blankets at night to keep them warm. Plus spending entire days two or three times a week away from earning a living. From mid morn into darkness. And sometimes knocked flat in a muddy ditch, horse scampered off, you'd be left distantly from civilisation, crying out into the cold air for help, unable to move.

You may assume by some of these more uncomfortable aspects of fox hunting that it's also a sport which in quick order sorts people out. And you'd be right. For no matter who they are or how they appear in civilian life they are all revealed true to their nature on the Irish hunting field. Separating in one dickens of a hurry the faint hearted from the brave, the quick from the laggard, and by god last but not least, the randy from the celibate. For when the blood's up and the adrenalin races through the veins and as you are suddenly confronted on all sides, and especially to the front of you, with the likelihood of instant maim or death and where, what courage, nerve or stupidity and obtuseness of which you are possessed, comes to prominence, you would be wont to think of leaving some surviving heirs. And at such times. Ladies hold on to your knickers. Gentlemen make room in your britches

For lust
By god
Upon this Irish soil
Lurks everywhere.

ANY GOOD DUBLINER IF NOT ABSORBED IN THE
MIDDLE OF A BOOK AS HE WALKS, WILL ALWAYS
BE SEEN WITH HIS NEWSPAPER SOMEWHERE UPON
HIS PERSON, ATTESTING TO PROOF THAT IRELAND
HAS ALWAYS BEEN AND REMAINS ONE OF THE
MOST LITERATE NATIONS ON EARTH.

XII

Now something you may not have realised in an anciently poor country such as this old Shamrock Isle where they don't want to let all the money out, is that there is a strategically located desk of somewhat modern design, but like a judgement seat which confronts at the end of a long hall all departing travelling passengers. And upon which it says in large blue letters

CURRENCY CONTROL

O dear. Panic. Fright. Confiscation. Fines. Imprisonment. In your pocket haven't you got wads of not only punts, which is the Irish name for a pound, but of dollars, Swiss francs and sterling and which you are spiriting out of this hard up nation. Ah but you would be walking by. Free as a leaf in the breeze. And blown constantly. And why? Because there is never anyone sitting there at the currency control desk. That's why. But the powers that be have at least let it be known and remind you of what you're getting away with. And now in the modern world it should be of no wonder to you that nowhere else on earth is the law administered with such consummated sophistication. Is it any surprise then that banks from all over kingdom come are rushing to open up. And although you may see a few native Irish go in and out of them, nevertheless all other kinds of ethnic persuasions are much in evidence. Which recently has given another aspect to this land which after all you've already heard will provide a shock.

Now straight off forget the likes of middle class old Dayton Ohio Harry and his well meaning wife Mabel. For in spite of all its old ways, believe it or not, Ireland is becoming by leaps and bounds a most glamorous country. This news is deliberately not being broadcast all over the place by those in the know, in case it crowds up where the private helicopters and aircraft are wont to land. The big old tumbling down mansions are being decorated, the dry rot hidden, the drips stopped dropping, and the lawns cut, and are again reverberating with the tinkle of glassware and solid clank of silver. The black tie and gowns again in evidence around the long mahogany tables. And the staff, mindful of the big salaries paid by these foreign millionaires, have not yet begun to kill the goose that's laying the present golden egg.

But as you might imagine among these folk not all of them are just merely wining and dining. And even in the face of the reputation of such a famously chaste place there do be other antics they do be pursuing. Not only joining with gusto in the lust of the fox hunt. But also with ladies and gents dismounted engaging in entwinements in the grass. And all aware in their wooing that it's a damn good way to consort with likely members of your exalted income group, if not make future friends for life. And what a wild and ready for anything bunch they are. Their palates primed for splendid sauces and the great wines. And nude by moonlight they become riders. Galloping the night away and ready to mount again the next morn. And indeed one lady returning after a day's hunting was overheard to comment as the groom remarked upon the condition of her stallion horse,

"Ah madam he do be having a fearful awful lather of sweat on him now."

"And so would you too my good man, had you been between my thighs all day."

Now as does the four footed ungulate, you'll have gathered that a sport such as fox hunting fits Ireland like a glove. The sad forlornness of the huntsman's horn sounding across the countryside. The peek of pink coming into sight upon distant emerald meadows. Cars adorned with emblems of the horse and none of your folk are ever without their sugar lumps to feed them. Even their haughty voices neigh. Children just out of the cradle are put in the saddle by their parents already crippled and maimed from riding injuries who stand now on their crutches smiling encouragement, as these youngsters are sent off screaming in fear with a resounding thwack on their pony's rear.

Now in Ireland a horse is never blamed for anything. If it kicks you in the head it only did so because you moved too suddenly and not suddenly enough to get out of the way. In short, horses are always forgiven and always beloved. And never mind the stallion that would eat its stable door down in order to bite off your goolies. And you would in your shocked hysteria, be expected to pet it back on the nose. And by god if only a horse could speak there would be even more libel and scandal spread aplenty. And perhaps there is a good enough reason for all this worship. For there is nowhere else that a lady, even of the plainest sort, looks better than on top of a horse. Bowler hatted, their hair coiffed in a net, their arses curvaceously to their best advantage displayed and supremely evident in tight britches in which thighs extend in clear definition over her mount's flanks. And is it any wonder that in such capersome recreation as fox hunting, that not only is the lady in hot pursuit of the fox, but frequently the Master of Foxhounds. Who often, poor old sod, finds himself waylaid in glades as well as bogs when he becomes the signal object of this venereal attention. And without doubt many a Master of Foxhounds is left feeling more like the hunted than the hunter. And frequently after a long day's chase interrupted by unchaste entwinements, Masters have been known to crash face first asleep into their soup over dinner. And by god you guessed it. Wasn't it the day herself the vicar's daughter radiant in pink coat no less, had just had her opening day out fox hunting with a vengeance.

But now we come to the moment of the year when all concerning this four hooved friend culminates in Ireland. And that would be in and during the social miracle of Horse Show week. And mind you, awful snobs that we are, we are not referring to your hoi polloi here. But to your green blooded Irishman with an occasional blade of grass growing up through his cap. And bog trotter or stud owner, low and high, and got up to the nines and desperate to be on their mettle during this, the most fashionable time of the year. And so, with riding and racing in all its forms pervading far more than just the open countryside, you'd expect to see a horse drawn dray or cab in Dublin. And if you be but just a wee bit patient you'll not be disappointed. Ah but there would be more. And it would be your incredible ilk of elegant people as can be witnessed nowhere else on earth. And although such is frowned upon by those who think they know better, expect as evening descends during hunting season to confront at your pub, hotel or Dublin cocktail party, a man returned from a day out, and still in his dashing rig with spurs clinking and burrs and thorns still sticking to his pink coat. He would of course be posturing conspicuously, prancing about, impatiently and continuously battering his thigh with his riding crop just to make doubly sure he attracted attention. Also too, although fewer in number, you'll find a notable traffic of polo players crossing the hotel lobby. These gents and some ladies, of the Mark II and III varieties, are easily recognised by the leather worn over the knees for protection. And damn me, while in their own very leathery unique gear, if some of them don't dare to stomp about dismounted with their mallets practising shots on the hotel carpet, especially where by tradition fox hunting fixtures are posted on the wall. And it wouldn't by god take old Dayton Ohio Harry long while just having an after dinner quiet brandy with Mabel, and still hanging around in Dublin looking for directions, to surmise that something frissonly saucy is about to be afoot further in the night up in the more discreetly remote rooms of the hotel.

"Holy cow Mabel I don't like the look of some of that leathery apparatus coming into this place. What the hell do you think is going on here?"

Now your old Harry is right to be agitated. For your

sure sign of your sadist equestrian like the one presently passing in the lobby, is the definitive manner in which his boot heels are brought thundering down on the floor with the accompanying tinkle of silver spurs. And conspicuously heard despite the thick carpeting. With the heads of the uninitiated turning. And especially poor old Dayton Ohio Harry who is now hot out of his seat exclaiming,

"Hey gee Mabel I sure don't like the sound of the jangle of those big long spikes on that guy's spurs. And holy cow see there, more leather goods being lugged into this hotel. And if that don't look like the trailing ends of a cat of nine tails to me, I'll eat my company tie. Holy mackerel, I'd sure like to know what in hell is going on. Just catch a glimpse of her will you."

Now unlike the bush by the tree in the fork in the road, concerning which Harry was advised by your country bumpkin, to take no notice, Harry is wide eyed apoplectic at what has just walked in. Nobody less than your English vicar's daughter. And thus is proclaimed the whole home-like intimate sociability of this land. For here she is the scarlet woman now seen casually loping by booted for riding and still in her hunting pink and with a rather ornate escutcheoned vasculum in tow, from which the highly adorned ivory handles of whips peek. Suddenly she stops, puts down the vasculum, takes off her hunting coat and slowly expands out her chest and yawns.

"Hey gee Mabel, gosh, is she built."

And is it any wonder that the vicar's daughter's newly purchased Ferrari has been safely housed in the grand safety and exclusivity of the Royal Irish Automobile Club not that far away up the street. And that she's abandoned her former al fresco activities and taken to the indoors to consort on a higher social and permissive level, and who knows, even a Protestant Catholic one. And now hasn't she, seeing that his eyes are dancing around in his head, even cast a brilliant friendly smile in old Harry's conspicuous direction. As in fact he has already jumped to his feet at the passing sight of her. As indeed, let me tell you, not only would it be her dazzling looks, splendid teeth and smile but doesn't she have a figure on her that would put a horn on Harry in a hurry. And bloody well bust any zipper ever invented on even the strongest fly.

"Sit down you stupid arsehole."

That of course was Mabel speaking. Which would at least remind you of the take no guff American variety of womanhood. And now you would also, from the previous reference to the emergence in Ireland of the female species of Man Fighter, be assuming it would be the woman whipping the man. Ah, thank god in this Shamrock Isle, nothing could be further from the truth. And certainly not during Horse Show week. But admittedly with her forthright stride the vicar's daughter does look as if she's going to be the one laying on the lash while mellifluously intoning,

"Take that. And that. And that. You naughty man."

Now as the astonishing circumstances would have it and as such is invariably the case in Ireland, aren't old Harry and Mabel located in the next ruddy room, to which your vicar's daughter is heading, albeit beyond a thick and soundly impenetrable wall. Harry out of his American mind with curiosity has enquired at the reception desk and has now rushed early to bed. But dutifully searching he's found a thin spot in the wall where old cupboards have been partitioned over in recent hotel decorations. Indeed the ruddy cavity is wonderfully working like a state of the art loud speaker. And of course old Harry has put two and two together as he clearly again hears the jangling of spurs, and gets a first hand insight.

"My god Mabel, this ain't no isle of saints and scholars, like is plastered all over the travel brochures."

"Well you, you pervert, are certainly aiding and abetting, listening through the wall, get back into bed."

"Hey honey I was just waiting for a scream in case someone had to rush to the rescue or something."

Recounting what Harry has just said is not for a moment to suggest that while the vicar's daughter and the Master of Foxhounds are enacting their little indoor horsey Gaelic ritual, that loud screaming is to be heard or indeed preferred. In fact quite the contrary is the case. For, among this element of Irish, and in this case the vicar's daughter of once-Irish, extraction, many generations previous to be sure, the ultimate frisson of subdued whimpering is regarded as providing the zenith of exquisiteness. Now of course Harry after being lost and bewildered ten solid head scratching days in the Irish outback is spending his very last tourist night in Ireland and, for a change at least, knows at last where he is, in his pyjamas with his ear pressed hard to the hotel bedroom wall. And with old Mabel, a Mormon originally from Salt Lake City, sporting a long impregnable nightdress, and admonishing a crouching on all fours Harry to get back into bed, he's finding his present entertainment much to his liking.

Now above all, simplicity of intimacy is one of the signal beauties of Ireland. And live and let live is the motto of the bigger and better Irish hotels. And on this stormy night nobody but the tourist likes of old horny Harry would be noticing in this top place what others are up to.

A SINGULAR COUNTRY

So now just as he is hearing faint female cries from the exquisitely delicious vicar's daughter and is now finding that more is the variety of the gentleman laying it on goodo across the lady's old whatfor, than it is of the lady's laying it on goodo across the gentleman's whatfor, now, on this dark evening, rain spattering the window, isn't he himself thinking of trying to be likewise with Mabel and he has this very moment removed his ear from the wall loud speaker, taken the leather belt from his trousers and told Mabel to lift up her heavy sleepwear curtain, and to put up her old whatfor bottoms up. Well as always is the case in Ireland, no one could have predicted what was going to happen next. For wasn't the Master of Foxhound's big arsed and ham handed lady wife this past moment coming soaking wet storming in the front entrance of the hotel making an almighty fuss at the discreetly conducted reception desk. And here she was now with the room number emblazoned on her mind rushing across the lounge between the vintage port drinkers, and into the hotel's back annexe. Pounding up three flights of stairs she is at this very moment rounding the corner from the landing and approaching down the hallway to arrive shouting, and fists raining and feet landing on the Master of Foxhound's door.

"I'll kill you. Kill you."

And for the oft repeated time one has to again admit that those old Anglo Irish are really full of your vim and vigour. Perhaps why some of them are, in these whipping activities, its greatest fanatics. And those devout in this practice might thank god that still one or two of your thick walled hotels have yet to disappear under the demolisher's hammer, quenching forever the low groans and satisfied grunts. As has now sadly happened in this present case with those emitting from your vicar's daughter under the presently administered chastisement of the Master of Foxhounds. For in addition to the awful kicking and thudding on the door next to Harry's comes a resounding crash. The M.F.H.'s wife having lifted up from the hallway floor a heavy bright red fire canister upon which was plainly stated

USE UPRIGHT
UNCOIL HOSE
RELEASE GUARD
STRIKE KNOB HARD
AIM AT FIRE BASE
USE ON ONLY CLASS A FIRES
NOT ELECTRICAL OR FLAMMABLE LIQUID
OR IRISH ONES

As a horsewoman herself the Master of Foxhounds' wife was strength personified and sent the fire extinguisher splintering through the door. Now Harry at that precise moment having landed a lash on Mabel's bottom, and hearing the almighty crash and thinking the vicar's daughter was trying to escape, and remembering vividly as to how she was built, wasn't Harry, suppressing his newly enjoyed sadism, suddenly overcome by an overwhelming attack of chivalry. And why not. For when it comes to gallantry there's no mopery let me tell you with your better class of American. But here now is the really surprising news. Isn't Harry in fact your first generation U.S.A.-born Irish. And still full of the new world's concept of courtliness and fair play. And back in the old sod to search out and find the thatched mud hovel wherein were born his ancestors and where, in and out of the parlour, did the chickens and pigs freely roam. So didn't he leave Mabel anticipating the next blow, which to her own surprise, she was looking forward to.

"Hey you jerk, where are you going?"

Although Harry had already learned plenty enough about the uniqueness of the Irish ways he knew by the destructive noise that something serious was amiss. And he was out in the hallway just as the Master of Foxhounds' wife disappeared charging into the darkness through the broken open door. The vicar's daughter lay nakedly prone upon the bed. The Master poised with his whip raised. And behind the wife in comes Harry as well. Still with his own belt in hand. The Master's wife, thinking Harry a bodyguard, gets behind a chair. And although Harry's in his pyjamas it must be said it was quite obvious he was in a highly erect compromised condition to be coming rushing into the Master of Foxhounds' bedroom. And anyone would be forgiven for thinking he was in the act of rape.

Now the big heavy canister of the fire extinguisher, and recently new to the country, contained a white foamy substance. Which, due to the uncontrolled wagging of its uncoiled hose, the released guard, and the knob being struck hard, was fast squirting and spraying a creamy froth in all directions. And especially blasted a splattering right into the face of Harry. Not only depriving him totally of his identity but also of a direction in which to proceed in order to protect a damsel in distress. At least temporarily he put the fear of god into the Master's wife with the Master himself shouting at Harry,

"Damn you man, who are you and what do you think you are doing?"

A SINGULAR COUNTRY

Now your Master of Foxhounds in his boots and spurs only, his whip unfurled, was long used to dispensing authority. But the whip was now grabbed from the Master by his wife. Who in an instant brought it down in one almighty lash across the vicar's daughter's bottom. Which Harry the potential rapist, wiping the foam out of his eyes was just in time to witness. And the vicar's daughter with an almighty scream jumped up standing on the bed and shrouded herself in the bedsheet. The Master of Foxhounds withdrawing into the shadows. The hose and nozzle of the extinguisher still oscillating as it continued to splatter spots on the antagonists and brighten up the hotel room's flowered wallpaper with its snowy white foam. And not an Irish soul occupying any of the other bedrooms in this old established hotel took a wit of notice of any of the unsociably sounding noise. But what was not known to anybody but the vicar's daughter was the presence, tucked in her vasculum, of her big eared toy Chihuahua dog, and as unIrish a canine as you could ever imagine considering the existence of the Irish wolfhound one hundred times its size.

"Woof woof."

Now everybody knew who the other was with the exception that nobody knew Harry. And in his present foam disguise, was not likely to. And to this cauldron of screams and shouts was added the high pitched barking yaps of this little mut as it jumped out to defend its mistress. And while Harry was dancing around wondering who to hit didn't he step directly on top of the tiny Chihuahua who with a squeal immediately started to try to bite hell out of Harry's bare feet. And who was already being given one awful belt in the kisser by the Master. Whose wife had mounted up on to the bed, grabbing and renting apart the sheet to which the vicar's daughter now desperately clung. Mabel meanwhile her own ear to the reverberating area of the wall, had telephoned what she thought was the hotel security but could only get room service.

"Ah now this time of night we've only got chicken, ham and cheese sandwiches."

"I'm not trying to order sandwiches. My husband's in a riot up here. I want the police."

"Ah madam you'd want to be ringing another number altogether for that."

Now in any other part of the world with the kind of imbroglio that was going on you'd have soon had your army and tank corps in attendance. But here on the Shamrock Isle you'd have to take into account the ever ready wonder of Irish hospitality. Hasn't your discreet Manager below, on the double had a table prepared with the "horse dovers" as they are referred to by the Irish in Erseland, plus attendant bottles of your various refreshment not excluding champagne. For wasn't the Manager and two acolytes from room service finally at the door, with the Manager intoning,

"Ladies and gentlemen, calm now if you please, if you will. Behave yourselves now please. There's a time and a place for everything. Haven't we refreshments to be served across the hall in preference to the Guards being called. Sure wasn't it all a misunderstanding and a mistake that any of us could have made, getting to the wrong bedrooms in the first place and all the time thinking they were the right ones."

Harry had a bloody nose. And the Master of Foxhounds under the onslaught of his wife, fled to another room given him free with the compliments of the Manager. And once more, without a particle of political or ethnic bias, the multi-orgasmic vicar's daughter with her vasculum, Chihuahua and tears in her eyes, descended by the lift with her whips to the lobby floor. And who should be there having a second brandy with his coffee and watching the hotel world go by, but Mr Ireland himself. His prayers already once answered by St Bridget and horny enough at this moment, to want to have them answered again. For in this intimate city of Dublin doesn't he know your vicar's daughter well and in a trice has her beside him over a drink. And sure wasn't she welcome to come back home with him with her dog and her whips. And upstairs while Harry had a pine scented foam bath, Mabel read the bible she found in a bedside drawer. But nothing would she find in this book more lenient and kind than the wisdom of Ireland. Which is everywhere like the rain. Falling with mercy and forgiveness. Especially where there is violent confusion, which, if it is ever straightened out,

Don't worry
There is plenty
More
Where that came
From.

THESE DAPPLED WATERS, OVER WHICH MANY A

SAD MAN HAS LEFT AND MANY A GLAD MAN

RETURNED, HAUNT THIS CITY WHERE THE

SEAGULLS STILL CRY AND SQUAWK OVER THE

ROOF TOPS.

XIII

With some of the nicest qualities still intact in the zodiac, what now is happening in this anciently emerald land? Where there are still samples of clean air to breath and pure water to drink. And in a word, plenty is happening. In a place providing for your social occasions galore. With your certified authentic international very top snob celebrities desperately seeking to come and be seen conspicuously strutting about and just being, like the natives, your ordinary flesh and bone human being, and not superior in the least. But you would be wrong to get the impression that Ireland nearly overnight has become a stamping ground for the worldwide rich. And just as well. For no more would your Bridget be curtseying or your Paddy be pulling his forelock to be at your beck and call in all their kowtowing guises.

But remember, for the sake of a pot to piss in, the bottom line never escapes your Irishman if there be but upon it written in black and white that there do be a quid or two to be pocketed of profit. For which he'll tolerate nearly any poison or rape any landscape. But beneath all his aesthetic ineptitudes he is a genius in dealing with the vicissitudes of life. Slow to panic when others do like scalded cats. And slow to wake up to see death on the doorstep with very Irish destruction on the way. Ready to wallow in sentiment or to become a bitter enemy or a fast friend.

And come here now a moment till I tell you. About where the young now swarm strumming strings. With a little elegance, and much less squalor. Few are older men who return to lament the dying of the mother. They walk strangers in the street. As new mummers and mimes tip toe past in frozen poses. Golden haired girls go by. A brown robed, sandal footed Franciscan friar strolls, sniffing the fragrance of Bewley's roasted coffee still hovering over Grafton Street. As once it was your most oriental of all cafés. A poet still stands guard at the gates. Within still plys a splendidly dignified waitress who comes in her black dress and white apron to your table. And in her nearly religious calling remembers back those months ago that you ordered cream for your black coffee, a spiced bun and butter.

And come here now another moment till I tell you. Ghosts up out of their graves again go walk stalking and glowering upon the pavements of this island's cities. Some still lurk there on the pavement. In their constant pain, grabbing pleasure where they can. They're there. They're everywhere. Amid drapery executives, gas meter readers, and the eternal tourists. Nothing new has happened that wasn't old already. Go down Dame Street. All those years ago. With only toothbrushes for luggage and the night ahead. Have another day of life. While the West's awake. In the glowering dark, a shouter goes by. He stops to point up. His words say to tell you.

"The stars are but big fading specks of dust in the distant sky."

And you listen to this knowledge. In this country where the songs born out of pain go singing. While upon this land where they are adored, the voices of children come. Out of the rainy cold of the winter shadows or in the calm stillness of a summer's eve. Here is where your self importance can achieve the heights. Provided you don't annoy the pooka. And where. If you love anyone

You can
Be their shamrock
In
The uttermost green.